AF892515

The New Australian Stockmarket Investor

The New Australian Stockmarket Investor

JOHN ENGLISH

ALLEN&UNWIN

First published in 2002

The information contained in this book is, to the best of the author's and publishers' knowledge, true and correct. Every effort has been made to ensure its accuracy. Neither the author nor the publisher accepts any liability for any loss, injury or damage caused to any person acting as a result of information in this book, nor for any errors or omissions. Readers are advised to obtain professional investment advice before acting on the information contained in this book.

Allen & Unwin
83 Alexander Street
Crows Nest NSW 2065 Australia
Phone: (61 2) 8425 0100
Fax: (61 2) 9906 2218
E-mail: info@allenandunwin.com
Web: www.allenandunwin.com

National Library of Australia
Cataloguing-in-Publication entry:

English, John W., 1944– .
The new Australian stockmarket investor.

3rd ed.
Includes index.
ISBN 1 86508 895 1.

1. Stocks—Australia—Handbooks, manuals, etc. 2. Securities—Australia—Handbooks, manuals, etc. 3. Investments—Australia—Handbooks, manuals, etc. I. English, John W., 1944– Australian stockmarket investor. II. Title. III. Title : New Australian stockmarket investor.

332.63220994

Set in 10.5/13 pt Janson by Midland Typesetters, Maryborough, Victoria
Printed by Griffin Press, South Australia

10 9 8 7 6 5 4 3 2 1

Contents

Figures and tables vii
Preface ix
Language of investing x

1 **Getting started** 1
Types of investments • Choosing a stockbroker • Placing your first order • Order execution • Settlement and transfer • Financial planners • Taxation • Investor protection

2 **Investment principles** 17
Establishing goals • Risk and return • Components of an investment strategy • Implementing an investment strategy • Monitoring performance

3 **Investment information** 33
Financial indexes • Newspapers and magazines • Company information • Stockbroker reports • Surfing the Web • Subscription services • Australian Stock Exchange • Sydney Futures Exchange

4 **Investing on-line** 47
Comparing services • On-line stockbrokers • Stockbroker web pages • Opening an on-line account

5 **Equity securities** 58
Features of equity securities • Investing for income • Investing for growth • Risk in equity securities • Searching for value

6 Fundamental analysis **75**
Top-down approach • Financial statements • Operating performance • Liquidity and solvency • Value indicators • Value versus price

7 Technical analysis **99**
Technical trading systems • Market indicators • Charting techniques • Artificial intelligence • Australian software suppliers • Australian data suppliers

8 Debt securities **117**
Features of debt securities • Rate of return in debt securities • Risk in debt securities • Interest rates and price volatility • Passive investment strategies • Active investment strategies

9 Derivatives **134**
Equity options • Buying a call • Buying a put • Selling a call • Selling a put • Warrants • Futures contracts • Futures trading

10 Managed investments **156**
Why managed investments? • Investment strategies • Unit trust products • Insurance products • Superannuation products • Cost of managed investments • Monitoring performance

Index **175**

Figures and tables

Figures

2.1	Economic clock	26
3.1	Australian Stock Exchange web page	44
3.2	Sydney Futures Exchange web page	46
4.1	Your Broker Online web page	48
4.2	BrokerChoice web page	49
4.3	Commonwealth Securities web page	52
4.4	E*Trade web page	53
4.5	Andrew West Stockbroking web page	53
4.6	Quicktrade web page	54
4.7	Rivkin Discount Stockbroking web page	55
4.8	E-Shares web page	56
5.1	Share quotation	63
6.1	Statement of financial performance	81
6.2	Statement of financial position	84
6.3	Statement of cash flow	85
6.4	Operating performance model	89
6.5	Present value	98
7.1	Daily bar chart	105
7.2	Candlestick chart	106
7.3	Point and figure chart	107
7.4	Moving averages	110
8.1	Standard & Poor's credit ratings	126
8.2	Riding the yield curve	132

9.1	Call option quotation	136
9.2	Buying a call	141
9.3	Buying a put	143
9.4	Selling a call	145
9.5	Selling a put	146
10.1	Personal Investment/Assirt Performance Tables	171

Tables

1.1	Dividend imputation	14
2.1	Investment risk	20
2.2	Asset allocation	25
10.1	Reasons for managed investments	158

Preface

In the 1990s, we had one of the greatest bull markets on record. Investors could throw their money at practically anything and make handsome returns. Sadly, that bull market ended and the investment environment has become more conventional. Nevertheless, there are plenty of opportunities to make money in the Australian stockmarket for those investors who are prepared to learn the essential skills.

If you want to learn about investing and you are not sure where to begin, this book will get you started. If you are ready to make your first investment, this book will answer your questions and aid you in making an intelligent, informed decision. If you are already an investor, this book will not only help to refine your investing skills, but also improve your ability to evaluate recommendations from stockbrokers and financial advisers.

The New Australian Stockmarket Investor has been written for the do-it-yourself investor. Its purpose is to equip you with the information that you need to take control of your own investment decisions. It is not a get-rich-quick book, nor is it a theoretical textbook. It is a practical book that has been written for individuals who are serious about investing their money in the Australian stockmarket.

Language of investing

The language of investing is part of the unique excitement of the stockmarket. It is intentionally colourful, sometimes dramatic and occasionally looks like a secret code. Learning the language is an important part of becoming an investor. The purpose of this section is to introduce you to the language of investing from the beginning, rather than treat it as a glossary at the end of the book. Have a look through the language of investing first, and then return to it whenever you find the words used and you want to refresh your understanding of what they mean.

Abnormal items Large gains or losses in a company's profit and loss account that don't occur in the normal course of business.

Accumulation index A share price index that assumes dividends are reinvested.

Active portfolio management A style of investment management that seeks higher returns. The opposite of *passive* investment management.

All Ordinaries Index A popular benchmark of aggregate changes in share prices that is used to monitor the Australian stockmarket.

American-style option An option that may be exercised at any time.

Annuity The payment of a fixed sum at regular intervals.

Arbitrage Buying and selling equivalent securities at the same time in different markets in order to profit from a difference in price.

Ask price The lowest price that sellers are willing to accept. Also called the *offer* price.

Asset allocation The systematic placement of funds into various classes of securities in a portfolio.

Asset backing See *net asset backing* and *net tangible asset backing*.

Associate company A company in which between 20 per cent and 50 per cent of its ordinary shares are owned by another company.

ASX A commonly used abbreviation for the Australian Stock Exchange.

At best An instruction to buy or sell at the broker's discretion as to price. Also called *at discretion*.

At-the-money When the exercise price of an option is equal to the market price of the underlying asset.

Australian Securities and Investments Commission (ASIC) The government corporate regulatory body for the securities markets.

Australian Stock Exchange (ASX) The financial market where listed securities are traded in Australia.

Authorised capital The amount of share capital with which a company is registered.

Averaging down Buying more of a security as its price falls.

Bank accepted bill (BAB) A negotiable discount debt security with a typical maturity of 90 or 180 days that is guaranteed by a bank.

Basis point One-hundredth of 1 per cent, the minimum unit of movement in interest rates.

Bear Someone who expects prices to decline. A *bear market* is a period of generally declining prices.

Benchmark An index or other measurement used to assess the risk and performance of a portfolio.

Beta A measurement of a security's volatility relative to the volatility of the market.

Bid–ask spread The difference between the bid price and the ask price.

Bid price The highest price that buyers are willing to pay.

Blue chip stock Shares in leading companies that are considered to be of high quality.

Board (of directors) A group of individuals elected by shareholders to formulate and direct a company's policies and objectives.

Bond A fixed interest security issued by the Commonwealth government or a semi-government authority.

Bonus issue Distribution of additional shares without charge on a pro rata basis to existing shareholders.

Book value The value of assets as recorded in the company's books of account. Book value *per share* is the total book value of the company's assets divided by the number of ordinary shares outstanding.

Books closing date The date on which a company closes its share registry to determine the shareholders who are entitled to a dividend, bonus issue or rights issue.

Bottom (out) The lowest price before the reversal of a downtrend.

Bourse The French word for stock exchange.

Breakout A price rise above a resistance level or a price decline below a support level.

Broker See *stockbroker*.

Brokerage Fees charged by a stockbroker for buying and selling securities on behalf of a client.

Bull Someone who expects prices to rise. A *bull market* is a period of generally rising prices—sometimes referred to as a *boom market*.

Business cycle The boom and bust pattern of economic activity.

Call A demand for money due on contributing shares or shares that are not fully paid.

Call option The right to buy a certain number of securities at a fixed price within a specific period of time.

Call provision A feature of some debt securities in which they may be retired or redeemed by the company before maturity.

Capital The funds invested in a company. Similarly, the funds an individual or fund manager has available to invest in securities.

Capital gain (loss) The difference between the price paid for a security and the price received when it is sold.

Capital structure The relative proportions of debt and equity capital in a company's balance sheet.

Capitalisation See *market capitalisation*.

Cash management trust A unit trust that invests in short-term money market securities.

Cash rate The current interest rate in the short-term money market.

Certificate of deposit A negotiable debt security similar to a bank accepted bill.

Charting See *technical analysis*.

CHESS The ASX *Clearing House Electronic Sub-register System* that is used to transfer listed shareholdings electronically.

Churning Excessive trading of a client's account by a broker in order to earn more brokerage fees.

Class of options Options of the same type (call or put) and style (American or European) over the same underlying security.

CLICK The ASX computer-based system used to trade options, similar to SEATS.

Client adviser A licensed individual that is employed by a stockbroker to advise clients and accept orders.

Close out To offset a currently held position.

Closed-end fund A fund that no longer accepts new investments. The opposite of *open-end fund*.

Commission See *brokerage*.

Congestion When the price of a security fluctuates within a narrow range.

Consolidated accounts Financial statement for a group of companies owned by a parent company.

Consolidation Combining a company's shares into a smaller number of shares, each with a correspondingly higher market value. Also called *reconstruction* or *reverse split*.

Contract note A document sent to a buyer or seller by a stockbroker confirming that a transaction has been completed and providing all of the details such as price, quantity and brokerage fees.

Contributing shares Ordinary shares that are not fully paid up.

Convertible Fixed interest securities or preference shares that can be converted into ordinary shares.

Correction A price decline after a period of rising prices. The opposite of a *rally*.

Coupon rate The rate of interest on a fixed interest security stated as a percentage of its par value.

Cover Cash or securities lodged by a client with their broker when buying on margin. Also, to close out a short position.

Covered option writing Selling calls while owning the underlying security, or selling puts while being short the underlying security. See *Short (position)*.

Cum dividend Shares that are trading with the buyer entitled to the declared dividend (trading *with* the dividend).

Cum rights Shares that are trading with the buyer entitled to the rights issue then current (trading *with* the rights).

Cumulative A provision in some preference shares in which any unpaid dividends are accumulated and payable before any ordinary dividends may be paid.

Day only An order that is cancelled at the end of the day if it is not executed. On the futures exchange, there are also *AM only* and *PM only* orders.

Day trader Someone who buys and sells in the same day.

Dealer A person who has a licence issued by the Australian Securities and Investments Commission to place orders to buy and sell securities.

Debenture A fixed interest security issued by a company and secured by a floating charge over all of its unpledged assets.

Debt security Loan securities, such as bank accepted bills, Commonwealth notes and bonds, debentures and unsecured notes.

Deferred delivery Shares quoted *dd* are the result of a reconstruction of a company's share capital that will result in a delay in settlement.

Deferred shares Ordinary shares on which dividend payments are not yet payable.

Delist Removal of a security from trading on the Australian Stock Exchange.

Delivery month The month in which a futures contract expires.

Delivery not enforceable Shares quoted *del* are the result of a new issue in which there will be a delay in settlement.

Derivative A security that represents a claim on an underlying asset, such as options and futures contracts.

Director See *board (of directors)*.

Discount The amount by which a security is quoted below its face or par value. The opposite of *premium*.

Discount broker A stockbroker who charges modest fees but who offers little or no extra services.

Discretionary account An agreement in which a client gives a broker the authority to trade the client's account.

Diversification Spreading a portfolio over a number of securities with the objective of reducing risk. See also *asset allocation*.

Dividend The part of company profits that is distributed to shareholders.

Dividend coverage Earnings per share divided by dividends per share, or the number of times the dividend is covered by net profit after tax.

Dividend imputation A tax credit attached to a dividend, known as a *franking credit*, for the company tax that has already been paid on the company's profits.

Dividend reinvestment plan A scheme whereby shareholders can elect to receive their dividends in shares, usually at a discount from the current market price, rather than in cash.

Dividend yield Annual dividends per share divided by the current share price.

Duration The investment horizon for a debt security in which interest rate risk is eliminated.

Earnings per share (EPS) Net profit for ordinary shareholders after tax divided by the number of ordinary shares.

Earnings yield Earnings per share divided by the share price. The inverse of *price-earnings ratio*.

Entitlement issue Equivalent to a non-renounceable rights issue that is often used by No Liability companies to raise equity capital.

Entry price The price at which a unit in a unit trust is issued. Also called *purchase price*.

Equity option See *option*.

Equity security Ownership in a company evidenced by shares.

Equity trust A managed fund that invests in shares.

European-style option An option that may only be exercised when it expires.

Ex dividend Shares trading with the seller entitled to the declared dividend (trading *without* the dividend).

Ex dividend date The date when shares change from being quoted *cum* dividend to *ex* dividend.

Ex rights Shares trading with the seller entitled to the rights issue then current (selling *without* the rights).

Ex rights date The date when shares change from being quoted *cum* rights to *ex* rights.

Exchange traded option See *option*.

Execute Completion of a transaction or a trade.

Exempt market A secondary market in which the securities of a specific company are traded outside a designated exchange.

Exercise To invoke the right to buy or sell the underlying security conferred by an option.

Exercise price The price at which an option can be exercised. Also called the *strike* price.

Expiration cycle The months on which an option class expires.

Expiration date The date on which an option expires.

Exposure Potential variation in the price or yield of an investment in a particular security or class of securities.

Extraordinary item A gain or loss in the profit and loss account from an item not usually associated with the normal activities of the company.

Face value The nominal or stated value of a debt security indicating the principal amount to be repaid at maturity.

Final dividend A dividend paid after the end of a company's financial year.

Financial futures A futures contract in which the underlying asset is a financial security.

Fixed interest security Negotiable debt securities issued by companies or government.

Float Raising capital for a company by public subscription.

Forward delivery Securities sold for delivery at a future date.

Franked dividend See *dividend imputation.*

Front-end load A commission paid to buy into a unit trust. See *entry price.*

Full-service broker A stockbroker who offers extra services and charges higher fees.

Fund manager A professional investment manager.

Fundamental analysis An attempt to determine the fair value of a security.

Futures contract A standardised contract to buy or sell an underlying asset at a price agreed to today for delivery in the future.

Gearing The proportion of debt capital in a company's capital structure. Also called *leverage.*

Gilt-edged Fixed interest securities that are considered to be of good quality.

Good 'til cancelled (GTC) An order that remains in force until it is executed or cancelled.

Growth stock Shares in a company with above-average prospects for future capital gains.

Hedge A transaction that protects against unwanted price movements.

Imputation See *dividend imputation.*

Index A number series used to measure broad changes in securities, such as the ASX100, ASX200 and ASX300.

Index bond A treasury bond that can either be *capital* indexed or *interest* indexed according to changes in the Consumer Price Index.

Index warrant A warrant covering one of the prescribed indexes of the Australian Stock Exchange.

Initial public offering (IPO) The first public sale of securities. See *float.*

Inside information Confidential information that is only available to a small number of people. Trading on the basis of inside information (*insider trading*) is illegal.

Institutional investor An organisation employing professional investment managers, such as life insurance companies, banks and unit trusts.

Intangible asset An asset that has no tangible or material form, such as goodwill or trademarks.

Interim dividend A dividend paid after the first half of a company's financial year.

Interim report A report on company operations for the first half of the financial year.

In-the-money An option with intrinsic value.

Intrinsic value A positive difference between the price of an option's underlying asset and the exercise price.

Issued capital The amount of a company's authorised capital that has been issued to shareholders.

Joint venture An agreement in which two or more parties jointly explore, finance, operate or invest in a venture.

Junk bonds Low-quality, high-risk fixed interest securities.

Leverage The process of increasing the funds available for investment by borrowing.

Limit order An instruction placing a limit on the highest price to be paid or the lowest price at which to sell.

Limited liability (Ltd) When an investor's liability is limited to the fully paid value of the shares held.

Liquid market A market in which a security can be quickly and easily converted into cash.

Listed security A security that is traded on the Australian Stock Exchange.

Long (position) Owning a security. The opposite of *short* (position).

Margin Borrowing by a client from their broker in part payment for the purchase of securities. In futures trading, a good-faith deposit required to be lodged when entering a contract.

Mark to market Settling margin variations as a result of price movement.

Market capitalisation The value of a company found by multiplying the number of shares outstanding by the market price.

Market order An instruction to buy or sell immediately at the best price currently available.

Maturity The date on which a fixed interest security is due to be repaid.

Merger A friendly takeover.

Minority interest The value of profits and equity that is attributable to the holders of interests in subsidiaries that are not wholly owned.

Money market A market in which financial institutions trade short-term debt securities such as treasury notes and bank accepted bills.

Mortgage A pledge over an asset to secure a loan.

National Guarantee Fund A fund maintained by the Australian Stock Exchange to protect the interests of investors if a stockbroker fails to complete a transaction.

Negative gearing A tax-reducing strategy in which the interest cost of borrowing exceeds the income earned from an investment.

Negotiable security A transferable security that can be bought or sold.

Net asset backing (NAB) Assets less liabilities divided by the number of ordinary shares outstanding.

Net asset value (NAV) Net asset backing per unit in an unlisted unit trust.

Net tangible asset backing (NTA) The same as net asset backing after deducting intangible assets.

New Recently issued shares are quoted as *new* when they don't yet rank equally with existing shares for dividends.

No liability (NL) Applied to some mining and oil company partly paid shares in which a call for the unpaid portion cannot be enforced. However, failure to meet the call can result in forfeiture of the shares.

Nominal value See *face value*.

Note A fixed interest security.

Off 'Change Transactions in listed securities that don't take place on the Australian Stock Exchange.

Offer price See *ask price*.

Official list Securities admitted to be traded on the Australian Stock Exchange.

Open-end fund A fund in which investors can buy and sell units at any time based on net asset value. The opposite of *closed-end fund*.

Open interest The number of outstanding derivative contracts for a particular class or series.

Open order An order that is good until it has been executed or cancelled.

Option Used in several ways:

- ***Company options*** are issued by a company and traded on the Australian Stock Exchange. They give the option-holder the right to buy new shares on specified terms for a period of time.
- ***Equity options*** are standardised puts and calls on existing listed company shares that are traded on the Australian Stock Exchange Derivatives market.

- ***Futures options*** are standardised puts and calls on financial futures contracts that are traded on the Sydney Futures Exchange.

Ordinary shares Units of proportional ownership in a company.

Out-of-the-money An option with no intrinsic value.

Over-bought The result of a recent price rise for which there is now an expected correction.

Over-sold The result of a recent price decline for which there is now an expected rally.

Over-the-counter (OTC) Trading via the telephone or computer screens that does not take place on an organised exchange. See *unlisted shares.*

Overweight Having greater exposure to an asset class than would be normal. The opposite of *underweight*.

Paper profit (or losses) Unrealised capital gains (or losses).

Par value See *face value.*

Pari passu A class of securities that has equal rights with another class of securities.

Partly paid shares See *contributing shares.*

Passive portfolio management A style of buy-and-hold investment management. The opposite of *active portfolio management.*

Penny stocks Speculative low-priced shares. Also called *penny dreadfuls*.

Play Jargon for a way to profit from an under-valued or over-valued situation.

Pooled investment Any form of investment in which individuals collectively place their funds with a professional investment manager.

Portfolio A selection of securities chosen according to an investor's goals.

Position A view on future market movements and/or an investment based on that view.

Preference shares Shares that have preferential rights over ordinary shares to dividends and assets.

Premium The amount by which a security is quoted above its face value, opposite of a *discount*. Also, the price paid for a put or call.

Price–earnings ratio (P/E ratio) Annual earnings per ordinary share divided by the current share price.

Primary market When securities are first issued and the funds constitute new capital to the firm. See *secondary market.*

Private placement The sale of securities directly to an individual or institutional investor without being offered to the public.

Program trading Orders that are automatically triggered when a computer recognises that certain conditions are present.

Property trust Pooled investments that specialise in real estate.

Prospectus A legal document issued by a company setting out the terms of its public issue of securities.

Proxy Written authorisation given by a shareholder for another person to vote their shares at a shareholders' meeting.

Punter A speculator who buys and sells frequently.

Put option The right to sell a certain number of securities at a fixed price within a specific period of time.

Quotation Prices at which buyers and sellers are prepared to trade. See also *ask price* and *bid price.*

Rally A price rise after a period of declining prices. The opposite of *correction*.

Ramping Jargon for attempts to artificially drive up the price of a security.

Ratings Indicators of the creditworthiness or riskiness of issuers of fixed interest securities.

Reaction See *correction.*

Realised profit (or loss) A profit (or loss) resulting from the liquidation of an investment.

Reconstruction A company may reconstruct its shares into units of greater value. Also called a *reverse split* or *consolidation.*

Redeemable Exchangeable for cash.

Reserves Shareholders' funds such as undistributed profits, capital gains and asset revaluations.

Resistance level A point at which an upward price movement is expected to slow down or stop.

Return Income and capital gains expressed as an annual percentage of the amount invested.

Rights issue A privilege granted to shareholders to buy new shares in the company usually below the current market price. *Renounceable* rights may be exercised or sold, *non-renounceable* rights may be exercised or left to expire but may not be sold.

Risk The chance that your realised rate of return will be different from your expected rate of return. See *volatility.*

Scrip Share certificates or fixed interest certificates that are evidence of ownership. Replaced by *CHESS* for listed shares.

Seat An old term that indicated membership of an exchange.

SEATS *Stock Exchange Automated Trading System*, a computer system that replaced floor trading on the Australian Stock Exchange.

Secondary market When existing (as opposed to new) securities are traded. Also called the *aftermarket.* See *primary market.*

Secured debt securities Securities that are covered by pledged assets.

Securities Evidence of ownership of bonds, debentures, notes or shares.

Semi-government bonds Fixed interest securities issued by state government-owned authorities.

Series Options of the same class that also have the same expiration date and exercise price.

Settlement and transfer Delivery of cash from the buyer and securities from the seller to complete a transaction.

Share A unit of equity capital in a company.

Share price index See *All Ordinaries Index.* See also *SPI.*

Share register The record of a company's shareholders.

Shareholders' funds The amount of accumulated capital and reserves in a company.

Short (position) Selling securities that are not owned with the intention of buying them back (covering) later at a lower price. The opposite of *long* (position).

Speculator An individual who accepts high risks in an attempt to earn large profits.

SPI Pronounced *spy*, share price index futures and options contracts.

Split Increasing a company's shares outstanding by distributing additional shares pro rata to shareholders.

Spread Buying or selling in one market or security and simultaneously undertaking the opposite position in another security or market.

Stag An investor who buys securities in a new issue with the intention of reselling them immediately at a profit.

Stamp duty A state tax on financial transactions that previously included the purchase and sale of securities.

Stapled securities Two different securities that are linked together and cannot be transferred separately, such as ordinary shares together with unsecured notes.

Stock See *securities.*

Stock exchange In Australia, the Australian Stock Exchange (ASX).

Stockbroker A firm that buys and sells securities for clients.

Stockmarket A collective term that includes trading in all securities irrespective of whether they are traded on an exchange or over-the-counter.

Stop-loss order An instruction to sell if a security's price falls below a specified level.

Straddle Simultaneously buying and selling different derivatives.

Strike price See *exercise price.*

Subscribe To buy securities being offered for sale in a prospectus.

Subsidiary A company that is owned or controlled by another company.

Support level A point at which a downward price movement is expected to slow down or stop.

Sweetener A feature in a securities offering, such as convertibility, that encourages investors to subscribe.

SYCOM The *Sydney Computerised Market* that replaced floor trading on the Sydney Futures Exchange.

Sydney Futures Exchange (SFE) The Australian market in which futures and futures options contracts are traded.

Takeover The acquisition of a controlling interest in a company.

Taker The buyer of an options contract. The opposite of *writer*.

Technical analysis Predicting future price movements from an analysis of past price movements.

Thin market Sporadic trading in a security caused by too few buyers and sellers, resulting in exaggerated price swings when trades do take place.

Tick or **Tic** The minimum change in price. Used primarily in bond and futures trading.

Time value The difference between an option premium and its intrinsic value.

Top (out) The highest price before the reversal of an up-trend.

Trader An investor who actively buys and sells securities over a relatively short time.

Treasury bond An interest-bearing debt security issued by the Australian government for maturities of up to fifteen years.

Treasury note A discount debt security issued by the Australian government for maturities of thirteen or 26 weeks.

Trust See *unit trust*.

Trust deed An agreement for the methods of receipt, investment and disbursement of funds.

Trustee security Securities that meet legal requirements relating to investments by trustees.

Underlying asset The asset subject to being bought or sold upon exercise of an option or delivery on a futures contract.

Underwriter A financial institution that assists in the issue of new securities by agreeing to purchase any unsold securities, thereby guaranteeing that they will be fully subscribed.

Unit trust An organisation that pools and manages investors' money by selling *units* in an investment trust.

Unlisted shares Shares that trade in the over-the-counter market and not on the Australian Stock Exchange.

Unsecured note Fixed interest securities that are not secured by a mortgage or other charge over a company's assets.

Vendor Seller.

Vendor shares Shares received by the seller in exchange for property sold to a company.

Volatility Degree of variation in the price or returns of a security. Measured by the annualised standard deviation. See also *beta*.

Volume Number of securities traded.

Warrant A long-dated option contract issued by a third party and traded on the Australian Stock Exchange warrant market.

Whipsaw Frequent buy and sell signals within a narrow price range resulting in numerous small losses.

Winding up The dissolution of a company in which the assets are liquidated to satisfy the creditors before any remaining funds are returned to the shareholders.

Writer A seller of options. The opposite of *taker*.

Yield The annual income from a security (interest or dividend) expressed as a percentage of its current market price.

Yield curve A graph showing the relationship of yield to maturity and term to maturity for a group of similar debt securities.

Yield to maturity The average annual return from a debt security purchased at the current market price and held to maturity.

Zero coupon bond A debt security that pays no interest but is sold at a deep discount from face value.

1

Getting started

TYPES OF INVESTMENTS 2
CHOOSING A STOCKBROKER 3
PLACING YOUR FIRST ORDER 5
ORDER EXECUTION 6
SETTLEMENT AND TRANSFER 8
FINANCIAL PLANNERS 9
TAXATION 12
INVESTOR PROTECTION 14

Becoming an investor begins by overcoming some of the fears that all new investors experience. Buying and selling securities generally involves the services of a stockbroker and this can be an obstacle for a new investor. Even those who get up the courage to make the initial contact may not go any further. Some people have the impression that they may not have enough money to invest and the stockbroker won't be interested in them. Others don't want to appear uninformed about the mechanics of investing. A few may even be afraid that they could be ripped off because they don't know enough about buying and selling securities.

The purpose of this chapter is to put you in the driver's seat. The types of securities that are traded in the Australian stockmarket, choosing a stockbroker and the mechanics of trading are introduced, followed by an examination of the services offered by financial planners, the effects of taxation and investor protection.

Types of investments

There are four types of investments—equity securities, debt securities, derivative securities and managed investments. Each represents a different way in which to invest your money, and each has its own risk and return characteristics.

Equity securities

Investors in equity securities are owners, and every public company must issue *ordinary* shares. A company may also issue other types of shares such as *preference* shares, *contributing* shares or *deferred* shares. Each differs according to the rights and benefits that it confers upon the shareholder. For example, preference shares generally take precedence over ordinary shares for the payment of dividends. Historically, shares have performed best for growth and protection against inflation. They offer potential for capital gains and dividend income as long as the company is successful. Shares are also susceptible to wide fluctuations in market price, however, and equity investors may suffer losses if the company experiences misfortune.

Debt securities

Investors in debt securities are lenders and, therefore, creditors. Debt securities are issued by governments, semi-government instrumentalities and companies. They include mortgages, bonds, debentures and notes. They promise to pay a fixed amount of interest on specific dates and to repay the principal amount on a maturity date. Debt securities may be long-term, such as twenty years, or short-term, such as 30 days. *Secured* debt securities are backed by the issuer's property, while investors in *unsecured* debt securities rely on the general credit standing of the issuer. Debt securities are generally considered a safer investment than equity securities because the issuer promises to repay the full amount at maturity and the interest payments are usually fixed and secure as long as the issuer remains solvent.

Derivative securities

A derivative security is a claim on another asset. Changes in the value of a derivative security flow directly from changes in the value of the underlying asset. Derivatives can be used to speculate in the underlying asset or to hedge against price changes in the underlying asset. Derivatives also offer a high degree of leverage. There are many types of derivative securities, including company options, exchange traded options, warrants, rights, futures contracts and futures options.

Managed investments

Managed investments are an arrangement in which individual investors' funds are combined into one portfolio that is managed by a fund manager. Managed investments are particularly attractive to small investors because they offer diversification and professional investment management. There are a number of ways in which managed investments are administered, including listed and unlisted unit trusts, insurance and friendly society bonds, and superannuation funds.

Choosing a stockbroker

A stockbroker is licensed to buy and sell securities for the public. The same firm, however, may serve the client either as a broker or as a dealer and they should always disclose the way in which they have filled, or *executed*, a client's order.

A *broker* acts as the client's agent. This means that they execute your orders to buy and sell securities. They neither buy from you directly nor sell to you from their own holdings. They charge a fee for this service and that is their compensation for handling the transaction. Securities that are listed on the Australian Stock Exchange (ASX) are almost always bought and sold for private investors by stockbrokers who carry out the transactions as an agent.

A *dealer* acts as principal rather than as the client's agent. A dealer buys from other dealers, brokers and clients, and they also sell from their own account. The dealer's profit or loss is the difference between the price they pay and the price they receive. Dealers are most active in unlisted securities, unit trusts, and securities that are offered to the public for the first time.

The public face of the stockbroker is the *client adviser* or the firm's representative. This individual provides the liaison between the client and the investment services offered by the firm. Many investors refer to the client adviser as their *broker*, but technically this is not correct. Client advisers are subject to an examination of their past career and their knowledge of investments before they can be licensed to accept orders from the public.

Finding a stockbroker is easy. Just look in the telephone directory or contact the Australian Stock Exchange. Finding a stockbroker and a client adviser that suits your particular needs, however, is a very personal decision. It is like choosing a doctor, an accountant or a solicitor. Ask your friends about their stockbroker, or talk to people like your banker, your accountant or your solicitor. A client adviser makes their living by helping you to invest your money. If you strike one that does not do the job to your satisfaction, then there are plenty of others. There is also nothing to stop you from having more than one stockbroker. There are a number of things to look for when you select a stockbroker, including:

- courteous attitude and quality service
- ease and promptness of communications
- efficient execution of orders
- amount and flexibility of brokerage fees
- quality and availability of research and advice
- financial planning and superannuation advice
- margin lending facilities
- fixed interest advice and dealing
- portfolio review and management services
- access to floats, managed investments, derivatives and foreign securities

Some stockbrokers specialise in particular types of securities, while others deal in nearly all types of securities. Some stockbrokers prefer to concentrate on large clients, and others base their business on small and medium-sized clients. It is important to weigh up the services offered and the fees charged before you choose a stockbroker.

At one end of the spectrum is the *full-service* stockbroker. They will spend the time to provide you with advice and information. A commission fee for buying and selling securities is the principal method of charging for stockbrokers' services. However, some stockbrokers want to reduce the emphasis on brokerage fees and charge separately for each of the services they provide. Stockbrokers set their own commission rates and they can charge different rates to different clients. Sometimes there is a sliding scale depending upon the amount of the transaction. A representative example would be 1 or 2 per cent of the value of a transaction subject to a minimum that varies between $30 and $100 per transaction. Brokerage rates are negotiable, so don't be bashful about asking for a reduced rate.

At the other end of the spectrum is the *discount* stockbroker. They charge the lowest commission rates, but they also provide the least service. Discount stockbrokers depend on volume to make money, so they simply take your order and don't give advice. Discount stockbrokers are particularly appealing to the do-it-yourself investor who does not need the services of a full-service stockbroker. Discount stockbroker commissions are generally between 0.1 per cent and 0.5 per cent, and minimum fees are as low as $16.

A recent development in stockbroker services has been the introduction of the Internet. Many full-service stockbrokers offer optional on-line services as a supplement to their existing services. However, most discount stockbrokers offer services that are designed specifically for on-line investing.

Placing your first order

Before a stockbroker can accept your first order, you need to open an account. The procedures are similar to opening a bank account. You will need to identify yourself and provide enough information to indicate that you are creditworthy. The stockbroker may ask you to deposit the required funds before taking your first order. If you want advice, you will need to discuss your financial circumstances and investment goals with a client adviser. Under Australian Securities and Investments Commission (ASIC) requirements, a client adviser must be able to demonstrate that they understand your circumstances and needs before making a recommendation.

To place an order, you first select the securities that you want to buy or sell. Instruct your stockbroker, either by contacting your client adviser or via the Internet, to execute an order for the amount you specify. The order is entered into the stockbroker's computer system and transmitted to the appropriate securities market—such as the Australian Stock Exchange, the Sydney Futures Exchange (SFE), or the over-the-counter (OTC) market—where it is executed at the best possible price. Confirmation of the executed order is reported back to you.

The simplest way to buy or sell securities is *at market*, which means that the transaction will take place at the market price that is prevailing at the time. Your stockbroker will always try to get you the best possible price. For example, you may wish to buy 1000 shares of XYZ Company that were last traded at $3.30. If you enter a market order to buy the shares, you could pay more or less for your shares depending on the best price your stockbroker can get when your order enters the market.

If you don't want to give your stockbroker discretion over the price, you can enter a *limit* order. A limit order to buy establishes the maximum price that you will pay. A limit order to sell establishes the minimum price that you will accept. When you enter a limit order, your stockbroker gets you the best price within the limit that you have set. If they cannot execute the order within your limit, then the order is not filled.

Order execution

Depending upon the type of securities that you want to trade, your order may be executed on the Australian Stock Exchange, the Sydney Futures Exchange or the over-the-counter market.

Australian Stock Exchange

Securities listed on the ASX are bought and sold using the computer-based Stock Exchange Automated Trading System (SEATS). The Australian Stock Exchange Derivatives (ASXD) market uses the CLICK system, which is the options equivalent of SEATS. All bids and offers at the same price are dealt with in the order in which they are entered into the system, regardless of whether they are large or small. Matching orders are automatically executed.

A glance at the SEATS computer screen will tell your client adviser where your order is in the system. The screen also shows the *depth* of the market consisting of the number of shares bid and offered at each price. It is possible for your client adviser to tell you how near your bid or offer is to the prevailing price and how many shares are ahead of you in the queue. The result is that your client adviser can assess the likelihood of an order being executed and advise you if the order should be changed or cancelled. In some cases, your order will be executed and confirmed before you hang up the phone.

Sydney Futures Exchange

SFE trading is conducted on the Sydney Computerised Market (SYCOM), which is a computer trading system linked to member firms' offices. SYCOM also enables clients in Europe and the United States to trade in Australian futures.

Over-the-counter market

The OTC market is a network of dealers who trade in securities that are not listed on an exchange. If you want to trade in unlisted securities, your stockbroker employs a different set of procedures to execute your order. First, the client adviser will transmit your order to the firm's OTC dealer. Typically, the dealer will contact another dealer that *makes a market* in that particular unlisted security. The dealers trade between themselves at a wholesale price and trade with the public at a retail price. Alternatively, your stockbroker may sell you securities that they already hold in their inventory. The mark-up on OTC securities is part of a stockbroker's remuneration for dealing in unlisted securities.

Settlement and transfer

Once an order is executed, the buyer's money needs to be exchanged for the seller's ownership in the securities. This is called *settlement and transfer*. It sounds simple enough, but behind the scenes is a complicated system of clearing transactions which ensures that the seller lodges the securities in deliverable form and the buyer pays for them with cleared funds. If you are buying shares, your stockbroker sends you a *buying contract note* that itemises the cost of the securities and the brokerage fees for executing the order. You must pay the amount of the contract note in cleared funds within three days. Your stockbroker advises the company's registrar of shareholders that you are now a shareholder. The company includes you on its mailing list for information regularly sent to shareholders, such as annual reports, notices of the annual general meeting and dividends. If you are selling shares, you receive a *selling contract note* and the proceeds of the sale.

Electronic settlement began with the introduction of *uncertificated holdings* in which shareholders in listed companies receive a holding statement that is similar to a bank statement instead of a share certificate. Because the system is electronic, the ownership of securities can be transferred instantly without having to rely on paper documentation. The flip side of electronic transfer is that *cleared* funds must be lodged with your stockbroker within three days of a purchase. Since it takes up to five days for the bank to clear your cheque, you need to deposit funds with your stockbroker in advance or arrange for the electronic transfer of funds from your bank account.

CHESS is the *Clearing House Electronic Sub-register System*. To use CHESS, you need to be sponsored by your stockbroker or financial adviser who will issue you with a *Holder Identification Number* (HIN). You quote your HIN to your client adviser whenever you place an order. Your HIN should be treated as confidential in the same way that you safeguard your bank PIN. If you want to have more than one stockbroker, then you will have a different HIN for each one. When you buy a parcel of shares through a particular stockbroker, you will need to resell them through the same stockbroker. If you want to change stockbrokers, however, your CHESS holdings can be transferred to another sponsoring stockbroker.

CHESS speeds up settlement and transfer. It also eliminates the proliferation of share certificates that arise from things like dividend reinvestment plans, bonus issues and rights issues, and it overcomes the problem of lost certificates. You receive a separate holding statement for each company in which you own shares. A statement is issued whenever the amount of the securities you own is altered by a transaction, including a listing of previous transactions during the year.

An alternative to CHESS is *Issuer Sponsored Holding*. This is also an electronic sub-register, but it is sponsored by the issuing company instead of your stockbroker. The company issues you with a *Security Holder Reference Number* (SRN) that you give to a stockbroker when you trade shares in that company. Treat the SRN as you would your bank PIN. The company sends you a holding statement for transactions in its shares. If you trade shares in many companies, you will probably find CHESS more convenient than issuer sponsored holdings.

Futures contracts and futures options are settled and cleared by the Sydney Futures Exchange Clearing House. There are no certificates issued, only a statement of the contracts bought or sold. The clearing house also determines the amount of the minimum margin deposit to be lodged for each contract that you hold.

Financial planners

Financial planners generally specialise in managed investments and retirement planning. They vary enormously in terms of their expertise and the services they offer. Not all financial advice is good advice, so it always remains your responsibility to evaluate both the advice you receive and the individual who is providing it. A financial planner should be prepared to offer you the following services.

- Review your current financial situation, including your cash flow, financial position, tax position, investments and retirement plans.
- Help you to identify and develop financial goals based on your circumstances and personal preferences.
- Identify key areas that will contribute towards improving your financial circumstances, such as budgeting, tax savings, upgrading investments or adjusting your superannuation strategy.
- Provide a written financial plan based on your goals, together with a realistic timetable for achieving them.
- Help you to implement your financial plan, including referrals to specialists, such as a lawyer or an accountant, if it is necessary.
- Regularly review your progress and suggest changes to your financial plan if any are needed.

Some financial planners are self-employed, such as independent operators, accountants and solicitors, whereas others work for organisations, such as financial planning companies, stockbrokerage firms, banks and insurance companies. Most financial planners earn all or part of their living from commissions on the products they sell. If you visit a financial planner, you will probably be asked to consider purchasing some of these products. The most dedicated, responsible and competent financial planner is, nevertheless, advising you to purchase investment products from which they will receive a commission. Be wary of this possible conflict of interest, thoroughly evaluate the recommendations yourself, and seek further advice if you need it. If you want to be sure that you are getting unbiased advice, look for an independent financial planner who works on a fee-for-service basis. Many financial planners offer a free first consultation, with subsequent charges ranging from $120 to $170 per hour.

Financial Planning Association

The Financial Planning Association of Australia (FPA) is the professional body for financial planners. There are three levels of members. The top level consists of the *principal members*, who are licensed dealers. They pass on their license authority to the *proper authority holders*, who are the individual advisers that deal with clients. The remainder are *general members*, who are yet to obtain practising member status.

Practising members belong to one of three categories—Associate, Senior Associate or Certified Financial Planner (CFP). Look for a CFP because they have fulfilled educational and experience requirements that are recognised as a professional qualification. They either charge a fee for advisory services, a commission on what they sell, or some combination of a fee and a commission. The FPA provides information about finding and choosing a financial planner.

A joint ASIC and *Choice* magazine survey suggested that there is a range of expertise in the financial planning industry. Of 100 financial planners surveyed, six achieved a *very good* assessment, 28 were assessed as *good*, 48 were rated *acceptable* and eighteen were *not acceptable*. Poor advice included lack of projections for cash flows, tax position, returns on investments and the client's future financial position. Of the 25 000 financial planners in Australia, the survey estimates that only one-third would qualify as CFPs. Financial planning is a relatively young industry that is working hard to raise its professional standards.

Master trusts and wrap accounts

Master trusts and wrap accounts are popular among financial planners. They consist of a service in which the administration and consolidated performance and taxation reporting for a range of investments is handled through one account. They vary tremendously in terms of costs and benefits.

A *master trust* is a managed investment product that invests in other managed investment products, giving you a number of fund managers through one investment. A *discretionary master trust*, also called *member choice*, allows you to choose the combination of managed funds that suits you. A *fund-of-fund* master trust is one in which you select the level of risk, and the master trust manager selects the combination of underlying managed investments for you. A master trust can handle superannuation funds or ordinary managed investments and it can be structured as a unit trust product or an insurance product. Fees are charged by both the master trust manager and the underlying fund managers.

A *wrap account* is an administration service that consolidates various investments under one umbrella, including managed funds, direct share investments, bank deposits, superannuation funds and allocated pensions. Unlike a master trust, assets are held in the name of the client instead of the trustee. Wrap accounts charge a variety of fees, including transaction fees and management fees.

Taxation

The Australian Tax Office (ATO) requires investors to keep records of their purchases and sales of securities. It is also in your best interest to keep good records in order to maximise the tax concessions that some securities offer. The effects of taxation on different types of investment earnings is briefly summarised here. However, you should seek professional advice from your accountant in order to determine how current tax laws apply in your particular circumstances.

- *Interest payments* from bank deposits, debentures, notes and bonds are included in your assessable income and taxed at your marginal rate. Be sure to quote your Tax File Number (TFN) if you don't want tax deducted at the top rate.
- *Dividends* from direct shareholdings are taxed at your marginal rate, but you may be entitled to franking credits depending on how much tax the company paid. You will be advised of the proportion of dividends subject to franking credits when you receive your dividends. Quote your TFN if you don't want tax deducted at the top rate on the unfranked portion of any dividends.
- *Capital gains* arising from the sale of securities (including shares, debentures, notes, bonds, options, rights and futures) are subject to capital gains tax. However, there are a number

of factors that can affect the amount of tax payable on a capital gain.

- *Income distributions* from equity trusts and property trusts are taxed. However, there may also be a flow-on of franking credits or depreciation allowances that make part or all of the distribution tax-free.
- *Tax concessions* are available to investors in particular types of investments under prescribed circumstances. These include insurance bonds, friendly society bonds, superannuation funds, rollover funds, allocated pensions and annuities, and pooled development funds. Professional advice is particularly important in assessing the after-tax effectiveness of these investments.

Capital gains tax

Securities acquired after 19 September 1985 are subject to a capital gains tax. This means you are taxed on any profits that arise from the sale of these securities. If they are held for less than one year, the total amount of the capital gain is added to your assessable income. If they are held for one year or more, then the way in which the capital gains tax is treated depends on when they were bought.

For securities bought after September 1999, one-half of the realised capital gain is included in your assessable income. For securities bought between September 1985 and September 1999, you can choose to subtract an adjusted *cost base* from the proceeds of the sale and include the difference in your assessable income. The adjusted cost base is determined by changes in the Consumer Price Index. Capital losses are not indexed. Capital losses can be offset against capital gains in the same or any future tax year, but not against income, such as salaries, wages, dividends or interest.

Dividend imputation

Dividends paid by Australian companies attract dividend imputation credits if the dividends are paid out of company profits on which company tax has been paid. These are generally referred to as *franked* dividends. The amount of the franking credit depends upon the amount of tax that the company paid. Some dividends have no franking credits. The company sends you a statement of your franking credits along with your dividend.

The amount of the dividend and the amount of the credit are added together (called *grossed up*). The grossed-up amount is taxed at your marginal rate and the franking credit is applied to determine the net tax payable. If you are on the top rate of tax, then you will pay some tax on fully franked dividends. If you are on a lower tax rate, you may actually receive surplus tax credits on fully franked dividends that you can use to reduce your tax on other income.

For example, suppose you receive a dividend cheque for $700 together with a statement indicating a franking credit of $300. Table 1.1 indicates the amount of tax that you will pay depending on your marginal tax rate on the grossed-up amount of $1000. Dividend imputation has significant tax implications for people in the top tax bracket who are considering shares versus fixed interest investments.

Table 1.1 Dividend imputation

Gross amount	Tax rate (%)	Gross tax ($)	Franking credit ($)	Net tax (credit) ($)
$1000	47	470	300	170
$1000	42	420	300	120
$1000	30	300	300	0
$1000	17	170	300	(130)
$1000	0	0	300	(300)

Investor protection

The ASX operates surveillance systems that ensure the integrity and stability of the market for listed securities. Surveillance systems help to maintain fairness and efficiency by focusing on any instances of inadequate disclosure by companies, trading rule breaches, insider trading and market manipulation. The ASIC also oversees the activities of the securities industry, including the ASX.

The National Guarantee Fund (NGF) is governed by the Corporations Law to provide protection for investors in the stockmarket. It is administered by the Securities Exchanges Guarantee Corporation. It is like an insurance policy in which the NGF provides no fault contract guarantees on all reportable transactions effected by ASX members in securities quoted on the ASX. It also affords some protection for investors against ASX members who may become insolvent.

The ASIC oversees the activities of the futures industry and regulates participants in accordance with the Futures Law. As a self-regulatory organisation, the Sydney Futures Exchange also oversees the activities of its members to ensure compliance with the SFE Business Rules and the Futures Law. The SFE maintains a Fidelity Fund to compensate clients who suffer loss in the event of misappropriation or fraudulent acts by an SFE member.

The *Financial Services Reform Act* came into effect in 2002. It provides for a number of requirements, including:

- disclosure of interests, fees and commissions that may influence advice
- suitability of advice based on a thorough knowledge of the client's needs and the products recommended
- disclosure of brokerage charges to clients
- advisory services guides for new clients
- warnings to clients about the applicability of general advice
- internal complaints handling processes in accordance with the Australian standard
- compulsory membership of an external complaints scheme
- special requirements in relation to dealing in derivatives
- increased training requirements for financial advisers

The best investor protection results from knowing yourself. When you invest your money in the stockmarket, you enter the financial risk–reward arena and submit yourself to a range of emotional pressures. Part of becoming an investor includes learning to recognise your motivations and feelings, particularly when you are on the verge of success or failure. Investment decisions are based not only on the analysis of information, but also on the personality, psychological mood and emotions of the investor. If you find yourself confronted by emotional reactions to your investments, recognise them for what they are and take steps to overcome them. Here are some suggestions:

- Don't even contemplate investing before you are sure that you can take care of all of your normal living expenses and obligations.
- Ensure that you fully understand the consequences if your first investment produces a loss.
- Increase your knowledge and understanding of basic economics and its effect on the prices and yields of securities.
- Develop your own investment goals and be sure that they are consistent with your knowledge, ability, financial position and emotional tolerance for risk.
- Re-examine your investments regularly, particularly in relation to changes in your responsibilities, income, age and investment goals.
- Remember that you cannot predict the future, but you can be sensitive to changing conditions that affect the securities you own.
- Be willing to take your losses when you are wrong without fear and without feeling guilty. Don't expect a miracle to bail you out of a declining stock or to put you on to a winner.
- Give special thought to long-term investing. It is usually more suitable for new investors, or for individuals who may be susceptible to excessive gloom or optimism.
- If you have substantial capital and an urge to speculate, then do it intelligently with a small proportion of your funds. A loss may cure your speculative itch forever.
- Try to avoid making emotional investment decisions. The market has long valued cool thinking during adversity as well as good fortune.

2

Investment principles

ESTABLISHING GOALS 18
RISK AND RETURN 19
COMPONENTS OF AN INVESTMENT STRATEGY 24
IMPLEMENTING AN INVESTMENT STRATEGY 28
MONITORING PERFORMANCE 31

There is more to investing than simply throwing your money at something and following what happens to it. An investment program consists of a logical sequence of events.

- Identifying the investment goals that you want to achieve.
- Determining the level of risk that is appropriate for your individual circumstances.
- Implementing an investment strategy that is consistent with your investment goals.
- Monitoring your investment performance and making periodic adjustments.

The purpose of this chapter is to describe a framework for investing. It focuses on fundamental concepts and principles that form the basis for developing your own approach to investing.

Establishing goals

There are two reasons why people invest. The first reason is to accumulate wealth. The second reason is to derive an income from the wealth that has been accumulated. Most individuals spend their entire working life trying to accumulate wealth. They may not recognise this as an investment goal, but it is nevertheless their primary financial objective. Undertaking a genuine investment program, however, requires goals that are more specific. Unless you have clear investment goals, how will you know which investments are right for you? Your investment goals will necessarily be tempered by your financial position, your age, your tax position and the amount of risk that you are willing to bear.

- *A sound financial position* and adequate income are important prerequisites for becoming an investor. Do you have ample provision for normal living expenses, some savings for emergencies, moderate debts and adequate life insurance?
- *Your age* is perhaps the next consideration in determining your investment goals. While there are no hard and fast rules, generally from the twenties through the forties the main objective is growth. During the fifties, growth is still significant but income becomes increasingly important. From the sixties onward, retirement income and avoiding risk are the main emphasis.
- *Tax effectiveness* will also be an important factor in shaping your investment program. The prospect of tax avoidance, however, should not be allowed to distort good investment judgement.
- *Your attitude towards risk* should be reflected in your investment goals. You assume some risk simply by deciding to be an investor. The question is how much uncertainty and possibility of loss can you withstand before you exceed your threshold for risk.

When you are clear about your circumstances, you are in a position to translate this information into investment goals. The objective is to establish the relative importance of three things—risk, income and growth.

- Avoiding *risk* is an important goal for everyone, but its importance varies according to your circumstances and your investment temperament. It means more than simply guarding the value of your investments. It also means protecting the purchasing power of your money against inflation.
- The amount and stability of *income* is important for retired individuals and others who need an income. The focus is on investments that reliably pay interest or dividends. The emphasis may be on interest-bearing securities or shares with regular dividends.
- *Growth* is important to people who are trying to accumulate wealth. There are different ways in which to pursue a growth-oriented investment program. One growth investor may follow a speculative growth strategy, while another may prefer long-term investments in high-quality stocks.

If your primary goal is income, then you want investments that provide interest or dividend payments regularly and dependably. If your primary goal is growth, then you want investments that are likely to increase in value so that they may be resold for more than their initial cost. If, however, your primary goal is to avoid risk, then you want investments that offer the greatest safety of principal and protection from inflation. Unfortunately, there is no single investment that simultaneously offers maximum income, maximum growth and minimum risk. These three investment goals are like the corners of a triangle. The closer you move towards one goal, the further you move away from the others.

Risk and return

The tradeoff between risk and return is the foundation for establishing investment goals. The obvious risk in investing is the chance that you may lose money. However, it also means that if you seek higher returns, you also bear greater risk. If you are not a big risk-taker, then you should be willing to accept lower returns.

Table 2.1 demonstrates the historical long-term relationship between risk and return for different classes of securities. An investment in cash securities such as treasury notes or bank bills

Table 2.1 Investment risk

	Chance of a negative return (%)	Long-term average return (%)
Cash securities	0	5.5
Fixed interest securities	13	6.5
Listed property trusts	15	7.5
Global shares	25	9.0
Australian shares	30	9.5

Source: Macquarie Investment Management

would have produced an average annual rate of return of 5.5 per cent with no chance of a negative return in any single year. Investing in listed property trusts would have produced an average annual rate of return of 7.5 per cent, but there would have been a 15 per cent chance of a negative return in any one year. Investing in Australian shares would have produced an average annual return of 9.5 per cent, but the chance of a loss in any single year would have been 30 per cent. The higher the returns you seek, the greater the risk that you may experience a loss in the short run.

Rate of return

The difference between the amount of money that you invest and the amount of money that you receive in the future is your profit or loss. It is referred to as the *return* on your investment. *Rate of return* is the percentage change in accumulated value between the time an investment is made and the time it is liquidated. It includes the capital gain (or loss) plus any cash flows from dividends or interest payments.

$$\text{Rate of return} = \frac{\text{Ending value} - \text{Beginning value} + \text{Cash flows}}{\text{Beginning value}}$$

For example, suppose you purchased shares for $20 one year ago. During the year you received $1 per share in dividends, and today you sold the shares for $25. Your rate of return is 30 per cent.

$$\text{Rate of return} = \frac{\$25 - \$20 + \$1}{\$20} = 30\%$$

In this example, you held the shares for exactly one year. However, investments may be held for periods that are more or less than one year. Unless the time frame is uniform, rate of return cannot be used to compare performance from one investment to another. Therefore, rates of return are generally stated on an *annualised* basis even though they may have been earned over some other period of time. The term *rate of return* is used in different ways.

- *Expected* rate of return is the anticipated rate of return that an investor thinks they will receive.
- *Required* rate of return is the minimum expected rate of return that an investor requires before they will invest.
- *Realised* rate of return is the actual rate of return that an investor receives.
- *Risk-free* rate of return is the return on an investment with virtually no risk. The interest rate on a Commonwealth treasury note is usually regarded as the risk-free rate of return.

Risk and uncertainty

Inasmuch as no one knows for sure what the future holds, investors face varying degrees of *uncertainty* about the rate of return for individual securities. A high degree of uncertainty causes investors to change their minds more frequently, resulting in increased trading and greater price *volatility*. There are several types of risk that contribute to the uncertainty about expected rates of return. They can be divided into three categories—risks that systematically affect all securities, specific risks that affect individual securities, and risks that are caused by the investor.

Systematic risks affect the returns of all securities, but they don't necessarily affect all securities in exactly the same way. They are external to the firm and cannot be controlled by the firm. Economic, political and sociological changes are the primary sources of systematic risk. Three important systematic risks are interest rate risk, inflation risk and market sentiment risk.

- *Interest rate risk* affects the returns from income and capital gains. When interest rates rise, the prices of income-producing securities fall. When interest rates fall, the prices of income-producing securities rise. Interest rate risk is particularly important when interest rates are high and unstable.
- *Inflation risk* affects the future purchasing power of investment returns. As a consequence, it also affects the prices of securities. Demand-pull inflation results from a shortage of goods and services during periods of full employment. Cost-push inflation results from an increasing cost of production. Both types of inflation causes the prices of goods and services to rise, which is reported in the Consumer Price Index.
- *Market sentiment risk* is a reflection of sweeping changes in investor expectations. It consists of broad fluctuations in market prices that can cause significant gains or losses. A dramatic example of market sentiment risk is the 1987 stockmarket crash that affected markets and investors around the world. Market sentiment risk is not simply a reaction to real events, but also to changes in expectations in which investors acting collectively may cause markets to overreact.

Specific risks affect the returns of individual securities. They are also called *non-systematic risks*. Three important specific risks are business risk, financial risk and market liquidity risk.

- *Business risk* is the uncertainty caused by the nature of the firm's operations and its competitive position. It is the degree to which the firm may become limited in its capacity to achieve its objectives. The ultimate business risk is failure. Business risk is reflected in changes in earnings per share.
- *Financial risk* is the uncertainty associated with the extent to which a firm borrows to finance its activities. Creditors rank ahead of shareholders for interest payments and distributions in liquidation. The larger the creditors' position, the less shareholders can expect. Therefore, changes to earnings per

share caused by business risk will be amplified by financial risk. A firm with no debt has no financial risk.

- *Market liquidity risk* reflects the ease with which securities may be traded without creating big price swings. When market liquidity is good, price volatility is reduced. When it is poor, it is called a *thin* market. A thin market is characterised by few buyers and sellers and a large spread between the bid price and the ask price. Market liquidity risk occurs in a thin market when it becomes necessary either to drop the asking price significantly in order to attract a buyer or to increase the bid price significantly in order to attract a seller.

Investor risks result from actions taken by the investor. Three types of investor risks are psychological risk, concentration risk and advice risk.

- *Psychological risk* results from an investor temperament that is susceptible to extremes of greed and fear.
- *Concentration risk* results from failing to diversify adequately in order to minimise the possibility of catastrophic loss.
- *Advice risk* results from selecting an incompetent adviser or acting on advice that is inappropriate, incorrect or biased.

Risk aversion

People generally don't like to take financial risks, and they can only be enticed to do so by the promise of greater returns. The more risk they are faced with, the less they like it. This is called *risk aversion.* However, individuals vary enormously in their degree of risk aversion, ranging from conservative to speculative. The important point to remember is that each of us has a different attitude towards taking risks; thus, recognising our attitude is vital in determining our investment goals.

The level of risk that matters most is the one you can live with when the market is sinking to new lows. Most investors are naturally optimistic at the top of a bull market and pessimistic at the bottom of a bear market. However, the big returns from stockmarket investing are based on buying at the market lows and selling at the market highs.

A rule of thumb for a moderate risk profile is to put 1 per cent of your portfolio into conservative investments for each year of your age. At 40 years of age, you might put 40 per cent of your portfolio into fixed interest securities, with 60 per cent devoted to shares. By the time you are 60 years of age, the proportions will have gradually reversed.

Components of an investment strategy

An investment strategy consists of five components. The first is *asset allocation*, or how your investments should be spread among various classes of assets. The second is *timing*, or how asset allocation decisions are affected by changes in the business cycle. The third is *asset selection*, or how to choose individual investments to include within each asset class. The fourth is *diversification*, or how to mix investments in order to minimise risk. The fifth is *liquidity*, or the ease with which investments can be bought and sold and the amount of cash reserves you decide to keep.

Asset allocation

Asset allocation refers to the proportion of investments you decide to hold in different asset classes depending on your overall investment strategy. Table 2.2 illustrates hypothetical asset allocations between cash securities, interest-bearing securities and shares for different investment strategies.

The *income* strategy has 80 per cent of its funds in cash and interest-bearing securities with only 20 per cent in shares. The *balanced* strategy has 50 per cent in cash and interest-bearing securities balanced by 50 per cent in shares. The *growth* strategy is 80 per cent in shares and 20 per cent in cash and interest-bearing securities. The *speculative* strategy consists entirely of shares. Asset allocation decisions are not fixed. As your investment goals change, your asset allocations will change as well.

Table 2.2 Asset allocation

Investment strategy	Cash securities (%)	Interest-bearing securities (%)	Shares (%)
Income	15	65	20
Balanced	10	40	50
Growth	5	15	80
Speculative			100

Timing

Asset allocation also depends on economic and market conditions at the time you are making your investment decisions. For example, you might be more interested in shares when the economy is growing vigorously and then switch to interest-bearing securities when the economy is sliding into recession. This ebb and flow of the economic tide is called the *business cycle*. As the business cycle moves from boom times to recession and back again, each asset class reacts differently. Figure 2.1 illustrates what happens as the business cycle sweeps around the *economic clock*. Understanding the economic clock is the key to investment timing.

The top of the business cycle occurs when the economy is booming. After it peaks and begins to slow down, interest rates rise and share values begin to fall. This is followed by falling commodity prices, tighter credit and, eventually, falling real estate values until the economy reaches the bottom of a recession. As the economy shows signs of recovery, interest rates fall and share values begin to rise. This is followed by rising commodity prices, easier credit and increases in real estate values until the top of the business cycle arrives again. Changes in interest rates are usually the trigger. Shares are the first to fall in a downturn and the first to recover when the economy improves. Real estate values tend to be the last to fall and the last to recover.

Figure 2.1 Economic clock

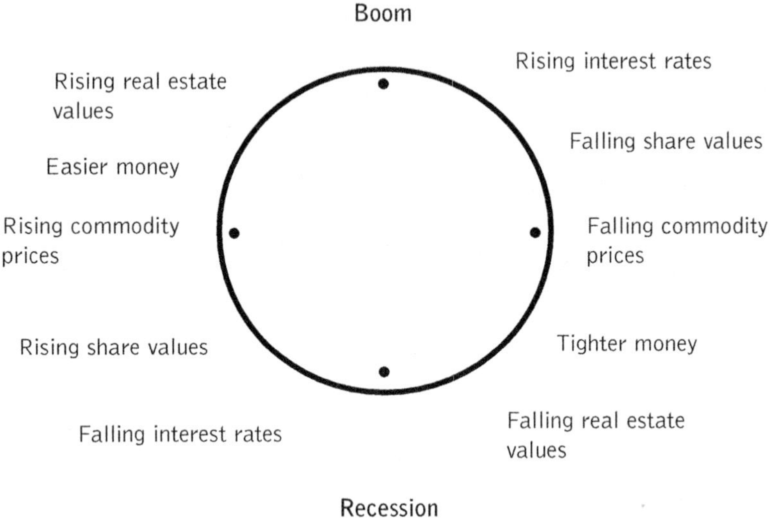

Asset selection

Asset selection is the process of identifying individual investments within each asset class. You can simplify the process of asset selection by using decision rules. Decision rules consist of defining criteria for accepting or rejecting individual investments. The process of defining decision rules is useful because it causes you to think carefully about what kind of investments you want. Once they have been defined, decision rules reduce the search time and the cost of finding suitable investment candidates by acting as a filter. Decision rules differ enormously from one investor to another depending on the type of investment program chosen and the amount of risk they are prepared to accept.

Diversification

Having a good mix of investments is an important issue. Diversification affords protection against near catastrophic loss if the market turns against any one of your investments. However, over-diversification produces only average results. An ASX share ownership survey revealed that 24.8 per cent of shareholders hold just one stock and another 27.5 per cent of shareholders hold only two or three stocks. This is important because it suggests that many investors are under-diversified.

Diversification is not just a matter of dividing your investment dollars among different investments. The key to diversification is to have a combination of investments in which each is affected differently by changing economic and financial market conditions. A reasonable degree of diversification can generally be achieved with eight to twelve stocks. The result is that the ups and downs for various investments tend to offset each other.

Concentration is the flip-side of diversification. It calls for limiting the number of investments to only a few that are carefully selected. Clearly, this is putting all of your eggs in one basket. If you are correct, you will reap the benefits. If you are not, you will suffer serious losses. Diversification versus concentration is important in the risk–return tradeoff. For most investors, the best approach is some form of selective diversification.

Liquidity

Market liquidity and cash reserves are an important ingredient in the design of your investment program. Market liquidity refers to a sufficient turnover of trading volume that enables buying and selling to take place easily and at a realistic price. Without market liquidity, you may have difficulty finding a buyer or seller willing to trade at the current price. Market liquidity can be measured by dividing the number of shares traded by the company's total issued shares. Market liquidity is generally greatest in the top 50 companies. As a rule, the market is less liquid for smaller companies and the shares of very small companies can sometimes go for days without trading.

Having some cash in reserve enables you to take advantage of sudden price breaks or new opportunities. Cash reserves are usually kept in the form of bank accounts, cash management accounts or very liquid interest-bearing securities such as bank bills. Cash reserves can be set aside from interest payments, dividends or the periodic sale of some of your investments. The amount that you decide to keep in cash reserves depends not only upon the investment environment, but also your investment goals.

Implementing an investment strategy

There are different ways in which to approach the components of your investment strategy. At one extreme is a passive approach in which you are not interested in spending too much time or effort in managing your investments. At the other extreme is an active approach in which you are intimately involved with every detail of your investment program.

A passive approach to investing consists of buying good-quality securities with no particular view about selling them in the future. The biggest advantage of passive investing is its simplicity. It also discourages inexperienced investors from needlessly or repeatedly changing their investments. The disadvantage is that a passive buy-and-hold policy simply fails to manage the investments. Under-performing investments are not replaced, profits are not harvested and the mix of investments may drift away from your goals. An alternative to passive investing is to invest in a managed fund and let a professional investment manager make the decisions for you.

An *active* approach to investing consists of changing the exposure between and within different asset classes in order to take advantage of emerging opportunities. If you decide to increase the exposure of one asset class beyond its usual allocation, then your portfolio is *overweight* in that asset class. Similarly, if the exposure to an asset class is less than its usual allocation, then it is *underweight* in that asset class. When a portfolio is actively managed, there may be times when it varies significantly from its usual asset allocation. An active approach to investing means continuously adjusting the asset mix to match your outlook for the economy, various industry sectors and individual companies. If your skill and judgement are good, then you should earn higher rewards. If your skill turns out to be poor, then active investing is more likely to produce losses.

An investment strategy is designed to achieve a particular investment goal. Investment strategies can be divided into income strategies, balanced strategies, growth strategies and speculative strategies.

Income strategy

The goals of an income strategy are safety of principal, a good yield and enough growth to offset inflation. Income strategies may focus on higher-grade interest-bearing securities, preference shares and very good quality ordinary shares that pay fully franked dividends.

Asset allocation in an income strategy is relatively constant. It is unlikely that the asset mix would be altered in reaction to temporary market moves. After significant market shifts, however, the portfolio would be readjusted. For example, if shares increased relative to interest-bearing securities, then readjusting would consist of selling some of the lower-yielding shares and using the proceeds to buy higher-yielding interest-bearing securities. Most income strategies are fully invested with little cash reserves.

An income strategy performs best when the investment environment is stable. It may lose ground in a strongly trending market or in the initial stages of a fundamental change in the investment environment. Of the four investment strategies, an income portfolio requires the least active management.

Balanced strategy

The goals of a balanced investment strategy are stability, an average income and enough capital gains to offset inflation and achieve moderate long-term growth. A balanced investment strategy may include quality ordinary shares, preference shares and interest-bearing securities. However, the proportion of equity investments is greater than for an income strategy.

Asset allocation decisions are based on anticipated future returns from different asset classes. A balanced investment strategy will generally ignore short-term market movements in order to benefit from longer-term trends. Changes to the asset mix are made on the basis of an assessment of the relative value of different asset classes. Over a full investment cycle, the portfolio weighting may alter significantly. Balanced investment strategies usually include some modest cash reserves.

A balanced investment strategy has the potential to avoid major downturns because it places emphasis on the relative value of different asset classes. It performs well in a rising market because it is realising capital gains and reinvesting the proceeds in under-valued assets. It may well under-perform, however, during a prolonged period of price decline. It takes a bit more effort to manage a balanced investment strategy than it does to manage an income investment strategy.

Growth strategy

The goal of a growth investment strategy is to realise significant capital gains over the medium to longer term. Income is not important. The way in which growth is pursued, however, depends upon the amount of risk that the investor is willing to accept. A growth investment strategy usually focuses on ordinary shares of varying quality. It is not unusual for a growth portfolio to experience significant volatility.

Asset allocation in a growth portfolio is based on an attempt to predict short- to medium-term market fluctuations. There are frequent changes to the asset mix. A growth investor needs to be prepared to completely change the asset allocation in order to protect the portfolio against short-term risk or to take advantage of a change in the investment environment. Growth portfolios typically maintain some cash reserves in order to take advantage of new opportunities.

A growth portfolio will achieve superior returns if the investor can correctly predict the market's reaction to events and take advantage of developing trends. A growth portfolio can also result in large losses, however, if the investor gets into a *whipsawing* market or if their predictions are wrong. A growth investment strategy requires active investment management.

Speculative strategy

The goal of a speculative investment strategy is maximum capital gains, with the least amount of invested capital, in the shortest period of time. A speculator is willing to accept very high levels of risk and has little concern for income, current business conditions or long-term trends. At different times, a speculative portfolio may have leveraged positions in interest-bearing securities, equity securities, rights, warrants, options or futures contracts. A speculator will probably pursue concentration as opposed to diversification, and they may be fully invested on some occasions and completely out of the market on others.

The fact is there are very few individuals who are genuine speculators. Most people have more conservative objectives, and if they speculate they do so with only a small portion of their funds. Ordinary investors simply cannot afford the time and effort that goes into managing a speculative investment strategy.

Monitoring performance

Whenever you go into a new investment, you should have in mind the amount of income or capital gains that you expect from it. This makes a good basis for evaluating the results. In fact, you should regularly evaluate the performance of each investment in your portfolio in order to determine where you got it right and where you did not. This will not only help you to make better investment decisions in the future, but it will also identify those parts of your portfolio that may need to be adjusted.

One way to evaluate your investment performance is to compare the rate of return for your portfolio with a benchmark like the Australian Stock Exchange All Ordinaries Index. Is your performance better or worse? Is your performance strongly or weakly correlated with swings in the stockmarket? How well does your portfolio perform in a good market? How well does it perform in a poor market? Keep in mind that your portfolio most likely represents a different asset mix than the All Ordinaries Index and your performance comparison needs to take into account the relative difference in risk.

In addition to monitoring your overall performance, you also need to evaluate the performance of each investment in your portfolio. The objective is to determine which investments you want to continue to hold, which investments you want to increase and which investments need to be sold. The performance criteria for individual securities can be as detailed as you wish depending upon the amount of time and effort that you are prepared to give to it. A good way to begin is to rank your investments according to their performance and your expectations. Then ask yourself, 'Why should I continue to hold an investment that I wouldn't be prepared to buy today?'

If *stability and safety* are your most important considerations, then high-risk investments with roller-coaster price volatility should be replaced with investments that are more reliable. If *income* is your goal, then investments with low or falling yields should be replaced with ones that have better yields. If your portfolio has been constructed for *growth*, then slow-moving investments should be replaced by ones with better prospects for capital gains.

3

Investment information

FINANCIAL INDEXES 33
NEWSPAPERS AND MAGAZINES 35
COMPANY INFORMATION 38
STOCKBROKER REPORTS 38
SURFING THE WEB 40
SUBSCRIPTION SERVICES 41
AUSTRALIAN STOCK EXCHANGE 43
SYDNEY FUTURES EXCHANGE 45

The process of investing is driven by information. Unless you have a professional interest in the financial markets, however, keeping fully informed is an impossible task. The sheer volume of information is beyond the capacity of any individual to thoroughly absorb. Nor is it always easy to locate the exact piece of information that you need in order to make a particular investment decision. It is important to be sufficiently informed to enable you to make your own investment decisions. In order to find investment information, you need to know where to look. The purpose of this chapter is to show you how to find the information you need.

Financial indexes

Financial indexes are used to measure broad changes in the value of securities in different sectors of the financial market. A *price* index reflects changes in prices only. An *accumulation* index reflects the reinvestment of interest payments or dividends as well, and measures the total change in accumulated value.

The ASX *All Ordinaries Index* is the most widely recognised stockmarket index in Australia. It consists of the largest 500 companies by market capitalisation, capturing nearly 99 per cent of the value of shares traded on the ASX. The *All Ords* is also a capitalisation weighted index, which means that larger companies have proportionately more effect than smaller companies. The top ten companies are equivalent to about half of the sample, and consequently movements in their share prices have a big effect on movements in the index. The All Ordinaries Index is divided into the *All Resources Index* and the *All Industrials Index*. These are further subdivided into a number of industry or market sector indexes.

ALL ORDINARIES INDEX

All Resources Index

- Gold
- Other Metals
- Diversified Resources
- Energy

All Industrials Index

- Infrastructure and Utilities
- Developers and Contractors
- Building Materials
- Alcohol and Tobacco
- Food and Household Goods
- Chemicals
- Engineering
- Paper and Packaging
- Retail
- Transport
- Media
- Banks and Finance
- Insurance
- Telecommunications
- Investment and Financial Services
- Property
- Health and Biotechnology
- Miscellaneous Industrials
- Diversified Industrials
- Tourism and Leisure

The All Ordinaries Index is the umbrella index for six *benchmarking* indexes.

- *ASX20* consists of the largest twenty companies on the ASX and is used to benchmark targeted investment strategies by institutions and large investors.
- *ASX50* consists of the largest 50 companies on the ASX and is used to benchmark similar strategies to the ASX20 but with a greater range of shares.
- *ASX100* is composed of the largest 100 companies and represents about 86 per cent of the market capitalisation on the ASX. It provides a benchmark for portfolios that focus exclusively on large companies with liquid share trading.
- *ASX200* is made up of the ASX100 plus another 100 stocks based on liquidity and represents about 89 per cent of the ASX market capitalisation. It provides a benchmark for portfolios that include a wider range of shares than the ASX100.
- *ASX300* consists of the ASX200 plus another 100 stocks based on liquidity and represents about 91 per cent of the ASX market capitalisation. It is used to benchmark portfolios that include smaller capitalised stocks.
- *Small Ordinaries Index* consists of the stocks in the ASX300 after removing the stocks in the ASX100. It is used to benchmark portfolios that consist of the shares of smaller companies.

Overseas share price indexes that are regularly reported in the Australian financial press include the *Dow Jones Industrial Index* (US), the *Standard & Poor's (S&P) 500 Index* (US), the *Financial Times 100 Index* (UK), the *Straits Times Index* (Singapore), the *Nikkei Index* (Japan) and the *Hang Seng Index* (Hong Kong). The Morgan Stanley Capital International (MSCI) World ex-Australia Index is a broad international index that accounts for about 60 per cent of the value of all companies listed on the exchanges of 21 of the world's largest markets.

Newspapers and magazines

Newspapers have, until recently, been the most timely and convenient source of investment information. Newspapers contain market quotations, general business news, financial opinion and financial advertising. *The Australian Financial Review* is Australia's only comprehensive daily financial newspaper. The financial section of the major newspapers, such as *The Age*, *The Sydney Morning Herald* and *The Australian*, also offer broad coverage.

The prices of many securities are published daily in the newspaper. Newspapers are not uniform, however, in the way they report price quotations. They also vary in the amount of information that they include in their market reports, such as earnings per share, dividends per share, dividend yield, dividend coverage, net asset backing and price–earnings ratio (P/E ratio). Mining and oil companies account for about one-third of Australian listed companies, which probably explains why they are quoted separately from industrial shares. In some newspapers, share transactions are also listed in a section called *Course of Sales* that reports each change in price that occurred during the trading day. In addition to share prices, major newspapers also carry quotations for futures, options, warrants, foreign exchange, interest rates and overseas markets.

There are a number of magazines and journals that publish investment information. In addition to general business and news publications, the following are especially useful.

- *Asset* (Fairfax Business Media: eleven issues per year) contains ideas, opinions and strategies for financial planners and other investment specialists. http://www.assetmag.com.au
- *Business Review Weekly* (BRW Media: weekly) is Australia's foremost business magazine. In addition to a wide range of business topics, it contains a great deal of current information that is relevant to private investors. http://www.brw.com.au
- *Ethical Investor* (Ethical Investor Pty Ltd: eleven issues per year) focuses on a variety of ethical issues related to investing. http://www.ethicalinvestor.com.au
- *JASSA* (Securities Institute of Australia: four issues per year) was previously known as the *Journal of the Australian Society of Security Analysts*. In addition to research, it contains views and information about matters affecting the securities industry. http://www.securities.com.au
- *Money Magazine* (APC: twelve issues per year) is the magazine spin-off from Paul Clitheroe's popular television show, *Money*.

- *Personal Investor* (Fairfax Business Media: twelve issues per year) is Australia's foremost investment magazine aimed at individual investors. Each issue consists of a number of feature articles plus a wide range of regular columns. http://www.personalinvestor.com.au
- *Shares* (Fairfax Business Media: twelve issues per year) is marketed with *Personal Investor* magazine and contains the Australian Stock Exchange Tables, which are updated monthly for all listed securities, plus market indexes. http://www.sharesmag.com.au

Newspapers and magazines are a rich source of information about broad economic and business trends. News items that reflect overall business conditions include reports about levels of production, retail sales, housing starts or changes in government policy. Other reports may reflect conditions in particular industries, such as exploration and production in the mining industry. Important items about individual companies include earnings, dividends, takeovers, new products, management changes, industrial relations and new financing.

Newspapers and magazines not only report factual information, they also publish opinion. Financial writers interpret economic developments, analyse trends, examine current developments and predict future prospects. When you read financial opinion, however, keep in mind that it can range from inspired prophecy to pedestrian axe-grinding. Some investors also make the mistake of thinking that investment information is only found in financial publications. Much of the general news also contains information that is relevant to investors. Here are some examples:

- international developments having an effect on world trade
- the imposition or relaxation of government regulations
- election speculation and the policies of the different parties
- new legislation and its effects on particular industries and companies
- actions of the Reserve Bank in respect of interest rates
- industrial relations and the effects on production, costs and sales

Company information

A good source of investment information is the companies themselves. A *prospectus* is a lengthy legal document that is issued when a company first offers securities for sale to the public. Its purpose is to present all of the information that investors and their professional advisers would reasonably require to make an investment decision. In addition to current financial information, a prospectus usually describes the company's plans for the future, including comments from independent experts.

Every public company is required to produce an *annual report* that, in addition to a great deal of window dressing, contains detailed audited financial statements. The annual report is the most comprehensive form of company information that is readily available to private investors. A number of other company reports may also be published, including half-year and quarterly interim reports, the chairman's address at the annual general meeting, other ASX announcements and investor newsletters.

Most listed companies have an Internet site. However, they vary tremendously in the scope and quality of the information provided. Some sites have a strong marketing or product bias. You can find links to many company Internet sites on the ASX web page (http://www.asx.com.au).

Stockbroker reports

Stockbroker reports have become important because quality research represents a competitive advantage for a stockbroker. Stockbrokers either reproduce reports that they buy from independent research firms or they publish reports that have been compiled by their own research analysts.

The job of the security analyst is to research developments that affect the companies they follow. They prepare reports on these companies that are distributed to the stockbroker's private and institutional clients. Some research reports concentrate on the analysis of a single company. Other more comprehensive reports may include the following topics:

- economic forecasts
- equity market theme
- equity market valuations
- equity market statement of financial position
- sector analysis for each industry group
- asset allocation recommendations
- forecast portfolio returns
- ranking of stocks by dividend yield
- ranking of stocks by P/E ratio
- stock selections and recommendations

Stockbroker reports have been losing credibility because their in-house analysts are sometimes caught in a conflict of interest. If a stockbroker is sponsoring a company in an initial public offering, then it will obviously recommend that you buy the shares. Similarly, when a stockbroker is earning advisory fees from a company, it is not likely that it will recommend a 'sell' on the shares. The lure of huge fees associated with corporate advisory work also means that any analyst who recommends a 'sell' on a potential client's shares not only risks the loss of future business from the company, but also the potential loss of their job with the stockbroker. Instead of using the word 'sell', terms such as 'neutral', 'market perform', 'downgrade' and 'hold' appear in stockbroker reports. Generally speaking, by the time a stockbroker's research reaches its smaller private clients, it has already been seen by their institutional clients.

When analysts make buy recommendations, how do you know which ones to take seriously? Most analysts don't consistently pick winners. One way to increase the odds in your favour is to look for stocks in which a number of analysts are making similar recommendations. These are called *consensus* estimates and recommendations. There is some research to suggest that consensus buy recommendations tend to identify stocks that perform above average. You can get consensus recommendations from specialist subscription services such as *Aspect Financial* and *The Inside Trader*.

Surfing the Web

Private investors can now get access to information that was previously only available to large financial institutions. With the development of the Internet, investment information is becoming easier to find and cheaper to obtain. Many Internet sites are designed for private investors. Some sites offer free information and others charge for their services. The most popular application on the Internet is exploring for information using the *World Wide Web*, or simply the *Web*.

To get on to the Web, you need a personal computer, an account with an Internet Service Provider (ISP), a modem connection and a *web browser* program. Most web users access the Internet with *Netscape Navigator* or Microsoft's *Internet Explorer*. Each website has a unique address (URL) that you type into the browser to retrieve it. A website URL begins with the letters http://www that tells the browser to use *hypertext transfer protocol* (http) and to search the World Wide Web (www). Hypertext is used to link websites together.

Hypertext words are highlighted, and when you click on one with your mouse you *jump* to another website that may be located anywhere in the world. Websites on similar topics are linked this way to enable you to find them. Jumping from site to site using hypertext has been termed *surfing* the Web. As you surf the Web, you will find sites to which you will want to return. You can use the *bookmarks* or *favourites* option in your browser to save these addresses so that you can easily find them again.

The remainder of the URL address contains the name of the website, its type and country location. The complete URL address for the Australian Stock Exchange is http://www.asx.com.au, for example. When you reach a website, you will be presented with its *home page*. The home page will offer you a *menu* of options that enables you to navigate to other pages in the website.

The best way to find sites that contain information on a specific topic is to use a *search engine*. A search engine is a continually updated index of the content on the Web. All you have to do is type in the *key words* that you are looking for and click on the *search* button. The search engine will tell you how many matches it found and display the first ten or twenty. When you find a site that interests you, you can click on its hypertext address and jump to it. To access a search engine, you type its Internet address into your browser. Here are some examples:

- Anzwers http://www.anzwers.com.au
- Alta Vista http://www.altavista.com
- Google http://www.google.com
- Infoseek http://infoseek.go.com
- Lycos http://www.lycos.com
- Webcrawler http://webcrawler.com
- Web Wombat http://www.webwombat.com.au
- Yahoo http://www.yahoo.com.au

Subscription services

Subscription services may be available in hard copy, by e-mail, or on the publisher's Internet site. They are a prolific source of investment information, recommendations and advice that is independently researched and evaluated. The following is a selection of some of the subscription services.

- *Australian Equities Research* provides a succinct analytical perspective on 130 of Australia's leading companies with regular company profiles, updates and financial results commentary. http://www.aer.com.au
- *Aspect Financial* is a specialist investor data provider that maintains an enormous database of information and analysis on almost all Australian stocks. http://www.aspectfinancial.com.au
- *BioTRENDS* and *CyberTRENDS* (Cyberstox: twelve issues per year each) are appropriate for investors who are interested in biotechnology stocks. http://www.cyberstox.com.au
- *The Bottom Line* (Assirt Equities: 52 issues per year) features in each issue an analysis of eight stocks, a market commentary and investment advice. See also the *shareanalysis.com* analysis and research reports on-line for most Australian stocks. http://www.shareanalysis.com

- *Fat Prophets* (Angus Geddes and Jason McIntosh: 52 issues per year) uses fundamental analysis to uncover undervalued stocks, and technical analysis to indicate timing. http://www.fatprophets.com.au
- *Financial Analysis Publications* maintains an extensive database of corporate profiles and financial information for all listed companies and many that are unlisted. http://www.fap.com.au
- *Huntley's Smaller Companies Guide* (Ian Huntley Publishing: 24 issues per year) provides advice on lower-priced shares. It is largely speculative in nature and seeks to identify those shares that have the potential for above-average returns. Updates are given on some twenty companies in each issue, including specific buy/sell recommendations as well as a Penny Share Portfolio. http://www.huntleys.com.au
- *Huntley's Your Money Weekly* (Ian Huntley Publishing: 48 issues per year) is a newsletter for the reasonably active stockmarket trader and investor, providing an insight into local and overseas economic factors affecting the share and commodity markets. It covers trends in mining, industrial and precious metals markets, as well as gas and oil exploration. Also, *Your Money Hotline* is a twice-daily three-minute recorded phone service. http://www.huntleys.com.au
- *The Inside Trader* (Personal Investment Planners: twelve issues per year) is based on a monthly compilation of the most recommended stocks of 23 brokers taken from around 600 stocks. See also *Stocks to Watch*, presenting short reports on ten highly recommended stocks for share traders. http://www.insidetrader.org
- *The Intelligent Investor* (The Strategy Forum: 26 issues per year) is an advertising-free sixteen-page newsletter with independent advice on what stocks to buy and sell. See also the *GTS Report* covering growth, technology and speculative stocks. http://www.intelligentinvestor.com.au
- *Thomson Financial Services Handbook* (Thomson Financial Publishing: annually) not only contains articles on financial markets, but also features a listing of hundreds of financial information

products and details about the organisations who offer them in Australia and New Zealand.
http://finance.tfp.com

- *InvestorWeb* has a database of financial data and reports on 600 stocks and 2500 managed funds.
http://www.investorweb.com.au
- *News and Views* (George Cochrane: twelve issues per year) is a four-page strategy newsletter for general investors. See also *Stockmarket Indicator* and *Buy'n Hold*, sixteen-page stock picker's newsletters based on technical analysis.
http://www.cochrane.net.au
- *Property Trust Monitor* (Property Investment Research: twelve issues per year) is an independent source of research and information on the Australian property trust industry, including both listed and unlisted trusts, syndicates and property securities funds. It contains analysis of current issues affecting property trusts, assessment of individual trusts, and explanations of issues such as valuations, new structures and taxation. http://www.pir.com.au
- *The Rivkin Report* (Rene Rivkin: 52 issues per year) is a popular newsletter from one of Australia's more colourful stockbrokers that specialises in stock picking.
http://www.rivkin.com.au
- *Shares Weekly* (Shares Weekly: 52 issues per year) is the online newsletter published by *Shares* magazine. *Shares Weekly* includes *Trendex*, which provides technical analysis for the share and options markets. http://www.sharesdaily.com.au
- Vaneyk.com (Van Eyk Research) have been the publishers of *Fund Watch* and *The Purvis Van Eyk Report*. They now offer a new interactive investment website with independent research and advice. http://www.vaneyk.com.au

Australian Stock Exchange

The Australian Stock Exchange offers investors a range of information and services. A good place to begin is the *ASX Information Source Guide*. It is a central location in which you can search for stockmarket information, products and services. The guide lists a number of information categories to make your search easier. Other features include links to stockmarket information distributors' websites. You can access the guide by visiting http://www.asx.com.au and clicking on the icon for *Investor Courses & Services* (see Figure 3.1) and then selecting the *ASX Information Source Guide.*

The ASX Internet site is one of the most popular investment sites in Australia because you can explore a vast range of information, products and services. The ASX Internet site contains information about the following topics:

- ASX and Australia
- ASX Charity Sharemarket Game
- ASX Investor Relations
- ASX/Employment Opportunities in Australia
- ASX/Dymocks Bookshop
- ASX Investor Education
- Information Source Guide
- ASX Careers

Figure 3.1 Australian Stock Exchange web page

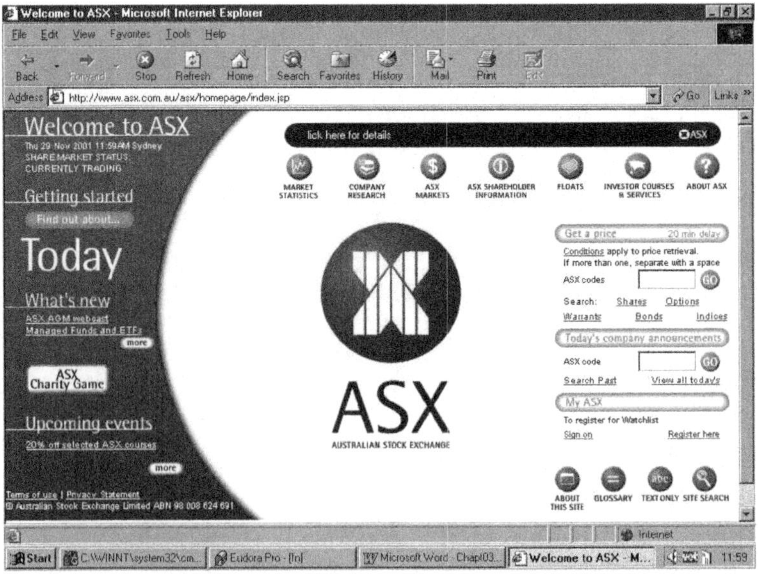

- The Information Centre
- How to Invest in Shares
- Broker Referral Service
- Simulated Trading
- Enterprise Market
- ASX Derivatives
- Companies
- Share Prices
- Glossary
- What's New
- Site Guide

Information on investing in shares is available in a step-by-step guide or as magazine pages covering topics ranging from buying and selling shares to maintaining a share portfolio. At the close of business each day, a market summary is available to keep you up to date with market movements, and the All Ordinaries Index is live on the site during ASX trading hours. You can also use the Broker Referral Service. By answering questions about the type of advice you are after, the area in which you live, or even the language that you speak, the service will provide you with the names of firms that can help.

Sydney Futures Exchange

A number of product brochures, publications and other services are available from the Sydney Futures Exchange (SFE) in Sydney or the Melbourne office. The SFE also maintains an extensive database and price history for each of the contracts traded that is available in hard copy, on disk or via the Internet. The SFE Education Centre provides courses, publications and information for people pursuing education, research and references for the futures markets. The resource collection consists of videos, files, journals and databases. The bookshop specialises in futures publications that it can make available through mail, telephone, fax and Internet requests. Tours and explanatory lectures for visitors are regularly conducted, and a number of courses are available through the SFE Education Centre. The SFE's Internet site at http://www.sfe.com.au is a one-stop shop for information about futures contracts and futures options (see Figure 3.2). It includes information about the following topics:

- Sydney Futures Exchange for a snapshot of the SFE, including its history, regulation, membership and trading hours.
- SFE Services for a list of publications available from the Resource Centre and information on SFE courses.
- Trading Futures and Options if you want to learn trading basics.
- Media Centre for fast and up-to-the-minute SFE news.
- Futures Contracts for information on the specifications for each of the contracts traded.
- Financial Services Directory for links to financial services organisations, regulatory bodies and associations.
- Market Data for current and historical data, including price, settlement, volume and open interest.
- SFE Clearing House for information on margins, fees and settlement procedures.

Figure 3.2 Sydney Futures Exchange web page

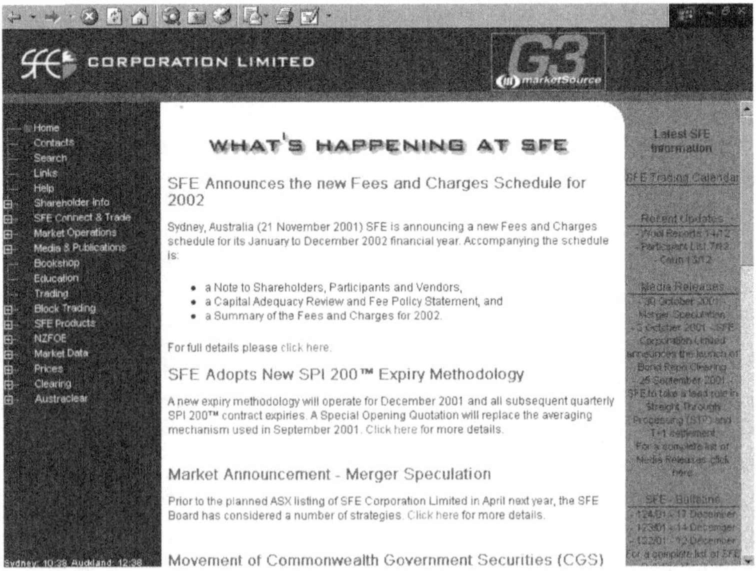

4

Investing on-line

COMPARING SERVICES	47
ON-LINE STOCKBROKERS	49
STOCKBROKER WEB PAGES	51
OPENING AN ON-LINE ACCOUNT	55

On-line investing accounts for about 20 per cent of the trades on the ASX and around half of private client transactions. Direct access to the exchanges, computer-based information, tools to manipulate and analyse vast quantities of data, and a variety of other on-line stockbroker services are available to suit the needs of individual investors. To take advantage of the benefits that on-line investing offers, you will need a personal computer, an Internet connection and an account with an on-line stockbroker. The purpose of this chapter is to investigate the nature of the services offered by on-line stockbrokers, how to compare them, and some examples.

Comparing services

On-line stockbrokers provide a wide range of services. Deciding which services are important to you is the first step in finding the best on-line stockbroker for your individual needs. Things move quickly in on-line broking and today's best-value service can be eclipsed by another broker in an instant. Among all of the features on offer, speed and reliability are the most important. However, there are a number of other features that you should investigate as well.

- What are the brokerage fees and are there and any discounts for frequent traders?
- In addition to ASX listed shares, is access available to other markets such as options, futures or managed investments?
- What trading tools are available, such as real-time market data, charting features or portfolio tracking routines?
- What research does the stockbroker provide on-line, including news services, ASX announcements and company profiles?
- How does your trading account operate, including the procedures for placing, confirming and processing orders?
- What type of cash account are you required to open to settle trades?

One Internet site that compares on-line services is *Your Broker Online* at http://www.yourbroker.com.au (see Figure 4.1).

Figure 4.1 Your Broker Online web page

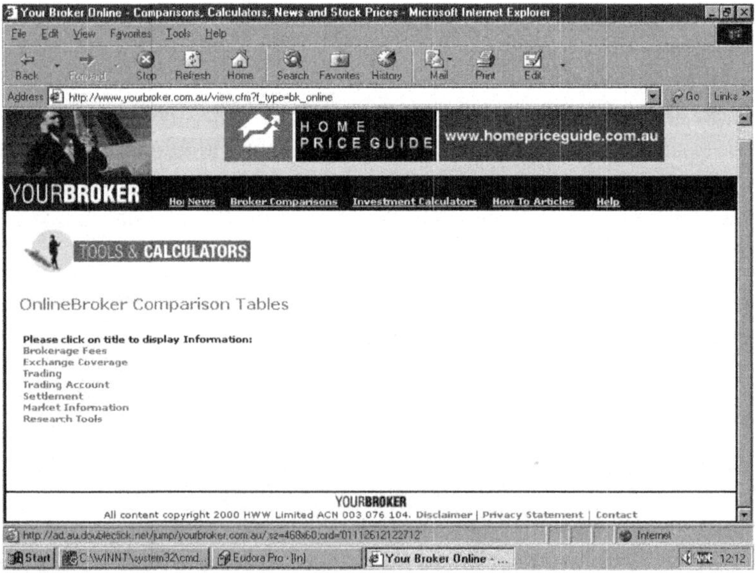

Another Internet site that compares on-line stockbrokers is called *BrokerChoice*. It can be found at http://www.brokerchoice.com.au (see Figure 4.2).

Figure 4.2 BrokerChoice web page

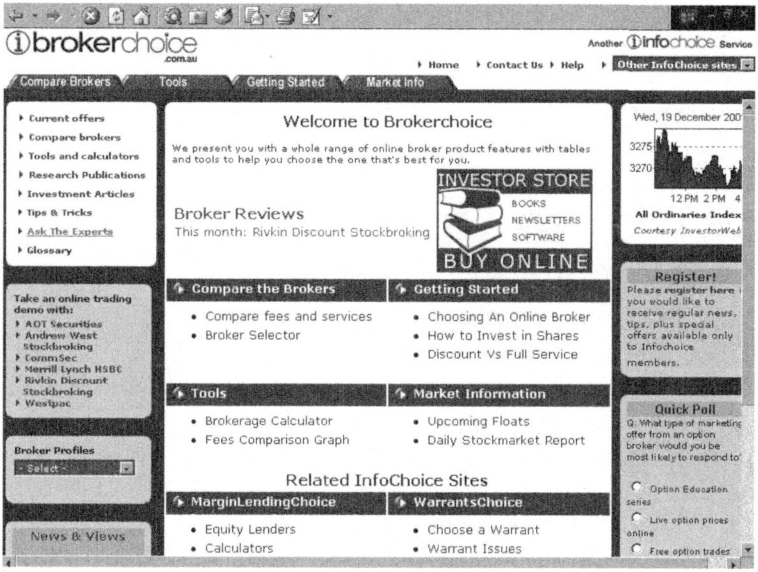

On-line stockbrokers

The following on-line stockbrokers are listed on the ASX website together with their contact information.

Andrew West Stockbroking
Telephone: 1300 136 323
http://www.andrewwest.com.au

AOT Online
Telephone: 1300 554 444
http://www.aotonline.com.au

Charles Schwab Pty Ltd
Telephone: 1300 360 383
http://www.schwab.com.au

Commonwealth Securities Ltd
Telephone: 13 15 19
http://www.comsec.com.au

Credit Suisse First Boston Australia Private Equities Ltd
Telephone: 1800 641 485
http://www.csfbaep.com.au

E*Trade Australia Securities Ltd
Telephone: 1300 658 355
http://www.etrade.com.au

Fleet Stockbrokers Ltd
Telephone: 1800 220 013
http://www.fleetstockbrokers.com.au

Macquarie Equities Ltd
Telephone: 1800 815 099
http://www.macquarie.com.au

Merrill Lynch HSBC Australia Pty Ltd
Telephone: 1300 308 938
http://www.mlhsbc.com.au

National OnLine Trading Ltd
Telephone: 13 13 80
http://www.national.com.au/trading

Rivkin Discount Stockbroking
Telephone: 1300 653 651
http://www.rivkinstockbroking.com.au

Sanford Securities Ltd
Telephone: 1300 360 892
http://www.sanford.com.au

TD Waterhouse Investor Services Ltd
Telephone: 1300 360 359
http://www.tdwaterhouse.com.au

Webstock Securities
Telephone: 1800 806 362
http://www.webstock.com.au

Westpac Broking
Telephone: 13 13 31
http://www.westpac.com.au

William Noall Ltd
Telephone: 1800 035 682
http://www.wnoall.com.au

Stockbroker web pages

Not all on-line stockbrokers offer the same range of services. The following selection is an example of the diversity of on-line stockbrokers.

Commonwealth Securities

Commonwealth Securities (CommSec) commenced trading in 1995 and is Australia's biggest on-line broker. CommSec emerged in response to increased share ownership in Australia and the availability of the technology for efficiently processing orders and settling transactions. The barriers to investing were lowered, with CommSec passing the savings from scale economies back to clients via lower brokerage.

Australian demand for CommSec's style of stockbroking business clearly existed among investors that were sceptical of the value offered by traditional brokers. That demand continues today in an expanded market as CommSec provides an accessible and affordable service, including Australian shares, international shares, managed funds, superannuation funds, margin lending, cash management account services, education centre, straight-through processing, research and access to new share issues (see Figure 4.3).

Figure 4.3 Commonwealth Securities web page

E*Trade Australia Securities

E*Trade is a large American financial services company. It is also Australia's second largest on-line stockbroker and it provides the on-line broking service for the ANZ Bank. E*trade offers brokerage services in shares, warrants and managed funds. It also offers clients news services and company profiles, and it has an arrangement with Morningstar Australia for managed fund profiles. Active customers have access to *Power E*Trade* which provides a number of valuable trading tools (see Figure 4.4).

Andrew West Stockbroking

Andrew West began in 1998 and is an example of a niche business in discount stockbroking and on-line trading. They aim to offer clients a truly personal service whether they trade with dealers over the phone or on-line. Services include Australian shares, managed funds, cash management accounts, straight-through processing, margin loans and research (see Figure 4.5).

Figure 4.4 E*Trade web page

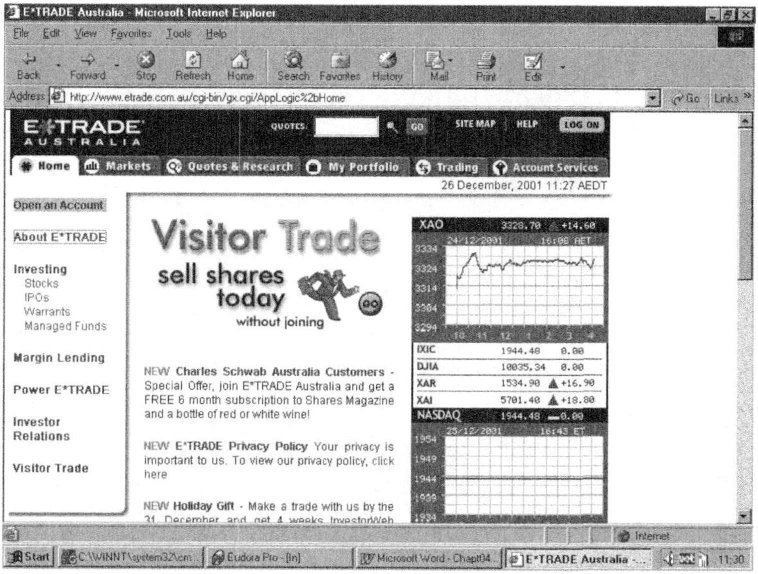

Figure 4.5 Andrew West Stockbroking web page

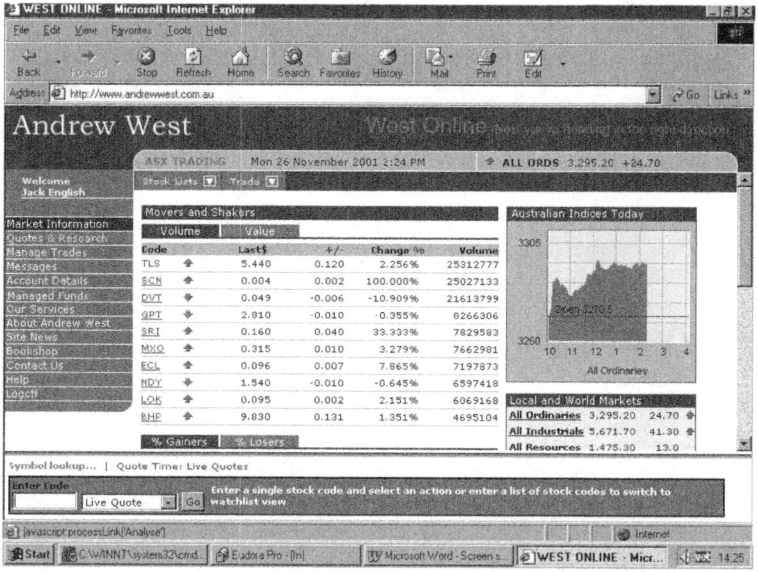

Quicktrade

Quicktrade is an example of a non-advisory trading service, with all trading and execution conducted by Merrill Lynch HSBC Australia Pty Ltd. Merrill Lynch HSBC does all the back office processing for Quicktrade with one of the best back offices in Australia. St. George Bank provides the banking services for Quicktrade. St. George also offers a full range of investment services, including margin lending, portfolio loans and cash management accounts. Quicktrade is part of Wealthpoint Limited, an ASX listed company (see Figure 4.6).

Figure 4.6 Quicktrade web page

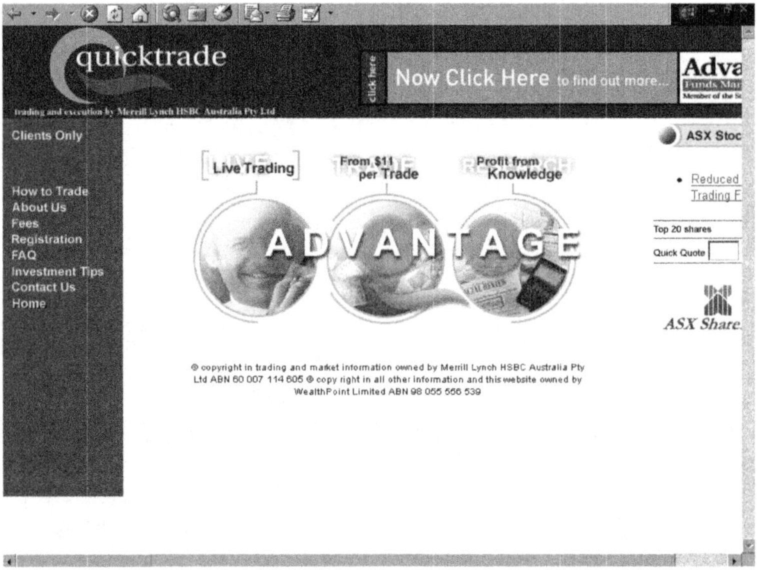

Rivkin Discount Stockbroking

Rene Rivkin is one of the investment community's most colourful characters and the Rivkin Discount Stockbroking (RDS) Internet site reflects Rene's presence. In addition to a biographical sketch of his life complete with pictures, RDS offers access to Australian shares, cash management account services, an education centre and margin loans (see Figure 4.7).

Figure 4.7 Rivkin Discount Stockbroking web page

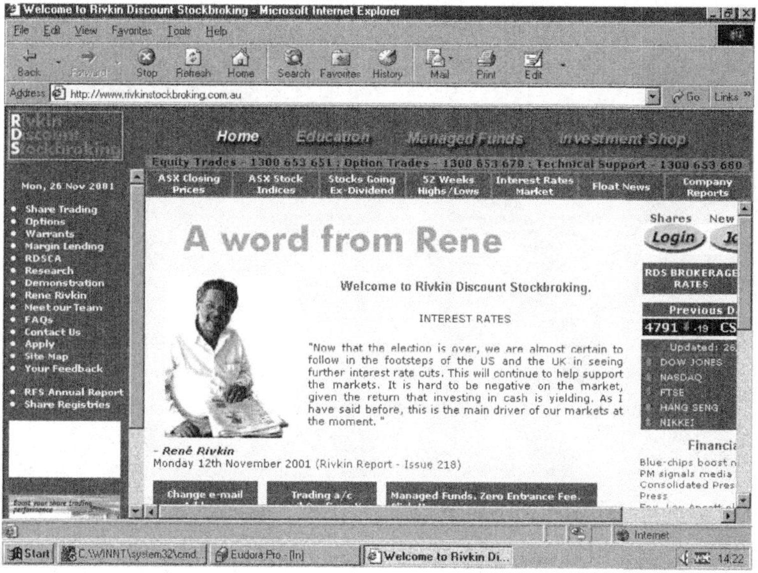

E-Shares

E-Shares is an example of an on-line broker with a particular interest in Internet-related businesses and high-end technology companies, including telecommunications, medical technologies, biotechnology and information technology (see Figure 4.8).

Opening an on-line account

Despite the fact that trading is done over the Internet, an on-line account is generally opened by filling out an application form and posting or delivering it to the stockbroker. Most brokers will ask you to deposit enough funds to cover your initial order. There are a number of extra features that you may want to consider as part of your on-line account:

- A cash management account for parking cash balances and clearing transactions.

Figure 4.8 E-Shares web page

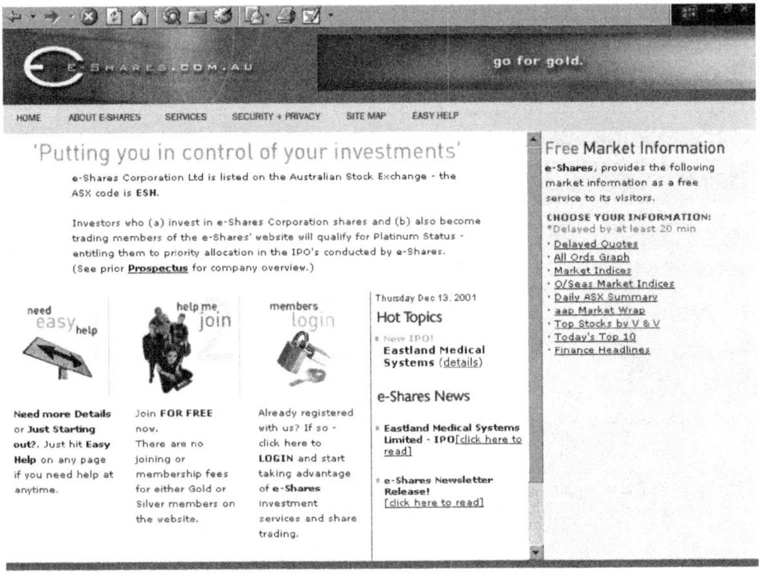

- A margin account, in which you can borrow to buy shares. Banks and brokers who operate this facility charge interest on the amount that you borrow.
- An option account. These are slightly more complicated and various rules apply. Option accounts differ depending on the type of option transactions in which you want to trade.

If you have an account with a traditional off-line broker and want to move it to an on-line broker, the procedure is quite simple. Ring the on-line broker and follow their instructions. For some on-line brokers you will need a cash deposit to get started; for others there is no such requirement. There is nothing to stop you from having accounts with more than one on-line broker.

All on-line brokerage services are at the mercy of the Internet's reliability. Ensure that your broker has a robust system and a reliable ISP provider. The reliability of your own ISP provider is equally important. Always ensure that you are running the latest version of your browser software.

On-line brokerage services depend on excellent customer service to attract clients. Even if you do all of your trading on-line, there are bound to be occasions when you need to telephone or e-mail your broker for assistance. You want to be sure that your on-line broker has well-trained and genuinely helpful staff who will assist you when you need it. The best test of customer service is the assistance you receive when you first open your account.

5

Equity securities

FEATURES OF EQUITY SECURITIES 59
INVESTING FOR INCOME 64
INVESTING FOR GROWTH 66
RISK IN EQUITY SECURITIES 67
SEARCHING FOR VALUE 70

Equity securities represent proportional ownership in a company. They consist of shares that can be transferred from one investor to another without affecting the existence of the company itself. Management control of the company is vested in a board of directors who are elected by the shareholders. As owners, shareholders have the opportunity to participate in the company's success through dividends and capital gains. Shareholders' financial liability, however, is generally limited to the amount they paid for their shares.

The purpose of this chapter is to describe the features of equity securities and how to go about searching for value in equity securities. The chapter begins with an explanation of the characteristics of different types of equity securities. It identifies the returns from income and growth and the tradeoff with risk. The chapter concludes with a discussion of some of the hiding places in which you can search for value in equity securities.

Features of equity securities

Equity securities are evidence of ownership in a company. Not all equity securities, however, are the same. They may differ substantially according to the rights they confer and the obligations they impose on the investor. Equity securities consist of two types—*ordinary* shares and *preference* shares. For each type, there can be more than one *class* of shares. For example, there may be 'Class A' and 'Class B' ordinary shares with differences in the rights that they confer on the shareholder. Shares can also be characterised in a number of other ways.

Shares may be classified either as *industrial* shares or *resource* shares. Industrial shares include manufacturing, retail and finance industries, whereas resource shares generally include the mining and oil industries. The ASX is somewhat unusual compared with stockmarkets around the world because one-third of ASX listed companies are in the resources sector. This reflects the nature of the Australian economy and it also makes our stockmarket more sensitive to commodity prices.

Some shares are regarded as *income* investments, whereas others are regarded as *growth* investments. Income shares pay large, regular and reliable dividends that give their shareholders a high dividend yield. Growth shares generally pay little or no dividends, but they are expected to increase significantly in price, realising a capital gain for the shareholder.

Shares can also be described as *blue chip* investments or *speculative* investments. Blue chip shares are generally associated with large, stable companies with a good reputation for profitable operations and regular dividends. Speculative shares are generally associated with smaller companies in which there is less certainty about future earnings.

Ordinary shares

Ordinary shares are the most common form of equity securities. Every public company has ordinary shares. Each ordinary share represents a fractional interest in the equity of the company. Ordinary shares confer a number of rights on the shareholder:

- A shareholder's financial liability is limited to the amount invested in a fully paid share.
- The right to a proportionate part of the company's profit each year. It is the board of directors, however, who determine if the profits will be distributed in the form of a dividend payment or reinvested in the company.
- The right to a proportionate part of the company's assets, after all of the debts are paid, if the company is wound up.
- The right to attend, speak and vote at company shareholder meetings.
- The right to receive prescribed information relating to the company.
- The right to sell the shares, including the right to accept or reject offers under proposed takeovers.

Contributing ordinary shares are only partly paid. For example, a contributing share may be issued at $3 with $1.50 payable on subscription and $1.50 payable at call. This means that shareholders are legally obliged to pay the remainder of the subscription price when the company asks them to do so. Shareholders in No Liability companies, however, may opt to forfeit their shares instead of paying the call.

Deferred ordinary shares are usually a separate class of shares in which no dividend is payable for a period of time. They are sometimes used to finance long-term projects in which the cash flows may not be realised for some time.

Ordinary shares were historically issued with a stated *par value* that was also referred to as *nominal value* or *face value.* Since par value bears no relationship to the market price or the fair value of a share, changes to the Corporations Law have resulted in shares with no par value for both existing and new companies.

Preference shares

Preference shares have a fixed dividend rate. Preference dividends must be paid before dividends on ordinary shares can be paid. Under certain conditions, however, the board of directors may decide not to pay the preference dividend. If the company is wound up, preference shareholders rank after debt-holders but ahead of ordinary shareholders in the distribution of liquidated assets. Preference shares come in a variety of forms.

- *Cumulative preference shares* accumulate the liability for dividends that may not have been paid. Ordinary shareholders don't receive ordinary dividends until the arrears in the preference dividends have been paid.
- *Non-cumulative preference shares* don't accumulate any liability for preference dividends that have not been paid.
- *Participating preference shares* have the right to receive additional preference dividends depending upon the company's profits.
- *Redeemable preference shares* may be redeemed under specified conditions.
- *Convertible preference shares* may be converted into the ordinary shares of the company under specified conditions at the option of the shareholder.
- *Converting preference shares* automatically convert into the ordinary shares of the company under specified conditions.

Company-issued options

Company-issued options are not strictly equity securities. However, they are a means by which an investor can indirectly take a position in a company's shares. Company-issued options enable the option-holder to take up new shares in the company at a fixed exercise price until an expiry date when the options lapse. Option-holders are not yet shareholders because they have not purchased the shares. The advantage is that for a small outlay option-holders can benefit from any increase in the share price. The disadvantage is that they have no voting rights or dividend entitlements. Company-issued options are occasionally offered as an incentive, called a *sweetener*, during a share float. They are usually traded on the ASX along with the company's shares.

Rights issues

Rights are not strictly equity securities either. Like company-issued options, they are a means by which an investor can indirectly take a position in a company's shares. Companies use rights issues to raise additional equity capital from existing shareholders. The rights permit existing shareholders to purchase additional shares at a predetermined price until an expiry date. The new share price is generally at a discount to the current market price and that gives the rights value. A company issues rights to shareholders in proportion to their existing shareholding. In a *renounceable* rights issue, the holder may choose to buy the new shares or sell the rights. Renounceable rights are generally traded in the stockmarket along with the company's shares. In a *non-renounceable* rights issue, the shareholder must either take up the new shares or forfeit the privilege.

The value of a renounceable right depends on the terms of the rights issue and the market price of the shares. Suppose that a company's current share price is $1.25. It has decided to raise more equity capital by issuing new shares for $1 each to existing shareholders on the basis of one new share for each four shares already held. Shareholders receive one right for each share that they hold. They have a choice between buying the new shares or selling their rights. They need four rights to buy an additional share for $1. If they sell the rights, their fair value can be calculated in the following manner:

$$\text{Value of a right} = \frac{\text{Share market price} - \text{Share subscription price}}{\text{Number of rights required} + 1}$$

$$= \frac{\$1.25 - \$1.00}{4 + 1} = \$0.05$$

Rights offer a leveraged claim to the underlying shares. If the shares in this example increased by 20 per cent to $1.50, then the rights would increase by 100 per cent to $0.10. On the other hand, if the share price fell below $1, then the rights would become worthless. Rights have a fixed life, so there is usually a premium for rights that don't expire for some time.

Reading the quotations

Share price quotations are reported daily in most newspapers, but not all newspapers use the same format. Industrial and resource shares are listed separately. The broadest coverage will be found in the major metropolitan newspapers and in *The Australian Financial Review*. Figure 5.1 is an example of a newspaper quotation for the Xeyez Company Ltd.

Figure 5.1 Share quotation

52 week High	52 week Low	Day's High	Day's Low	ASX Code	Company Name	Call Code	Last Sale	+ or –	Vol 100's	Buy	Sell
5.35	3.55	5.13	5.06	XYZ	Xeyez ...	1234	5.13	+7	4775	5.11	5.14
1.49	1.25	1.39	1.37	XYP	Xeyez pref...	5678	1.38	+1	25	1.38	1.40
.25	.05	.21	.20	XYR	Xeyez rts...	3456	.21	+4	225	.20	.22

- The first line is for the ordinary shares, the second line is for the preference shares and the third line is for the rights.
- The first two columns are the highest price and the lowest price during the previous year.
- The next two columns are the highest price and the lowest price during the day's trading.
- The *ASX Code* is used to identify the shares in the ASX computer system.
- The *Company Name* is usually shortened or abbreviated.
- The *Call Code* is a four-digit code that can be used to obtain real-time telephone quotations during trading hours.
- The *Last Sale* is the closing price for the day, followed by the net change (+ *or* –) in price since the closing price on the previous day.
- *Vol 100's* is the number of shares traded, or trading volume, expressed in multiples of 100.
- The *Buy* column is the highest-price bid at the close of trading.
- The *Sell* column is the lowest-price offered at the close of trading.

You will also find another listing of share price quotations called the *Course of Sales*. Its purpose is to report how the price of each share changed during the day's trading together with the trading volume. Some newspapers also include quotations for overseas shares.

Investing for income

When a company is profitable, the ordinary shareholders have a right to share in the profits in proportion to their shareholdings. One way in which ordinary shareholders may share in the profits is the payment of a cash dividend. The board of directors decides how much of the profits will be paid out in dividends. Companies generally pay dividends twice each year. The first is a smaller *interim dividend* paid after the middle of the financial year. The second is generally a larger *final dividend* paid after the end of the financial year. In a particularly good year, the directors may also declare an *extra dividend.*

When a company declares a dividend, it specifies an amount to be paid per share to shareholders who are listed on the company's share register on the *books closing date*. The shares will be traded and quoted *cum dividend*—with the dividend. Three business days before the books closing date, the shares will be traded and quoted *ex dividend*—without the dividend. When the shares go ex dividend, the buyer is no longer entitled to the dividend, and the share price will generally fall by the amount of the dividend. Dividend information is reported daily in the *Dividends Declared* column of *The Australian Financial Review.*

The *dividend yield* is the dividend per share for the past year as a percentage of the current share price. Dividend yields for individual shares are reported with the share price quotations in *The Australian Financial Review*. Dividend yields are particularly important to income investors and the top-yielding shares are regularly reported in the financial press. For example, if a company paid dividends of 25 cents per ordinary share over the past twelve months and its current share price is $5, then the dividend yield is 5 per cent.

$$\text{Dividend yield} = \frac{\text{Current annual dividend}}{\text{Current share price}} = \frac{\$0.25}{\$5.00} = 5\%$$

Keep in mind that some companies pay fully franked dividends. This raises the possibility that a low dividend yield which is fully franked may offer a better after-tax return than a higher dividend yield that is not franked.

The proportion of earnings paid out in dividends is called the *payout ratio*. For example, if a company earned 50 cents per share and paid a cash dividend of 20 cents per share, then the payout ratio would be 40 per cent. The payout ratio is one way of measuring a firm's dividend policy and comparing it with other firms and industry averages. It reflects the directors' judgement about how much of the company's profit is paid to shareholders and how much is reinvested in the business.

A company's dividend policy is an important benchmark for investors because it determines the income stream from investing in the shares. Over the past twenty years, nearly half of the returns to equity investors have been the result of reinvested dividends. Investors also use dividend announcements as information in assessing share value. Sudden changes in dividend policy tend to cause swift changes in share price, and the market's reaction to unfavourable dividend announcements is generally greater than for favourable announcements.

Some companies offer a *dividend reinvestment plan* in which you can elect to receive all or part of your dividends in company shares rather than cash. Shares distributed in this way are usually issued at a discount to the ex dividend share price and the transaction costs are absorbed by the company. The main advantage is that it is an inexpensive and convenient way to accumulate more shares. For the company, it represents the effective sale of new equity and the conservation of cash. Some companies, however, have been suspending or eliminating their dividend reinvestment plan because they have discovered that increasing the number of shares in this way dilutes earnings per share and may actually depress the share price.

The main reason that some investors choose preference shares is the certainty of dividend income. Preference shareholders rank ahead of ordinary shareholders for a fixed dividend and return of capital. In return for greater certainty, preference shareholders generally give up their claim to participate in the company's profits.

Investing for growth

A capital gain occurs when an investor sells shares for a price that is greater than the original cost. There are two principal methods used to identify potential capital gains. They are called fundamental analysis and technical analysis. *Fundamental analysis* is concerned with establishing the fair value of a share. Investors using fundamental analysis look for shares that are selling for less than their fair value. *Technical analysis* is concerned with market timing and price patterns. Investors using technical analysis look for signals that indicate when to buy or sell.

Fundamental analysis

Fundamental analysis is an attempt to determine a share's fair value. If fair value is greater than the share's current market price, then you may want to buy the shares in anticipation of a capital gain. Fundamental analysis can be approached in two ways—the growth approach or the value approach.

The *growth approach* says that companies with above-average earnings growth will produce share values that result in above-average capital gains. The objective is to identify companies with significant potential for future earnings growth before it becomes reflected in the share price. Recently, the growth approach has included a focus on smaller companies, known as *small caps*, that have few shares outstanding and the potential for rapid earnings growth. Investors who adopt the growth approach are looking for shares with the following characteristics:

- above-average P/E ratio
- below-average dividend yield
- above-average price to net tangible assets

The *value approach* says that there are times when a company's share price can be depressed simply because it is out of favour. For example, investors may be avoiding one company's shares because the market appears to favour another company. With few buyers and many sellers, the share price becomes too low relative to expected earnings and the fair value of the shares is greater than their current market price. Investors who adopt the value approach are looking for shares with the following characteristics:

- below-average P/E ratio
- above-average dividend yield
- below-average price to net tangible assets

Technical analysis

Technical analysis is an attempt to determine when and how a share's price is likely to change. It is based on the assumption that history repeats itself. Those who engage in technical analysis include chartists and quantitative analysts who specialise in the investigation of share price cycles and patterns. Technical analysis can be approached in two ways—the market timing approach and the price pattern approach.

The *market timing approach* says that a company's share price will fluctuate within a normal range. The objective is to buy the shares when the price is near the bottom of its normal range and to sell them near the top of its normal range. In more sophisticated versions, the normal range may be adjusted for other influences such as changes in the business cycle.

The *price pattern approach* says that share prices tend to produce chart formations that recur. Changes in price patterns are the result of shifts in the balance of supply and demand for the shares. A familiarity with past price patterns can be used to predict future share price movements. Some very sophisticated techniques have been developed to analyse and predict share price patterns.

Risk in equity securities

In order to gain some perspective about risk in equity securities, recall from Chapter 2 that risk can be divided into those risks that systematically affect all securities and those risks that only affect specific securities. The objective is to find ways in which to compare shares on the basis of risk. Three ways to approach comparing risk is the P/E ratio, the beta factor, and the differences in risk between shares in small versus large companies.

Price–earnings ratio

The P/E ratio is the most widely used approach to quantify the tradeoff between risk and return for shares. It consists of today's share price divided by the earnings per share for the past twelve months. For example, if the closing price of a share is $4 and earnings per share for the past year have been 25 cents, then the P/E ratio is 16.

$$\text{P/E ratio} = \frac{\text{Price per share}}{\text{Earnings per share}} = \frac{\$4.00}{\$0.25} = 16$$

Changes to the P/E ratio are essentially driven by fluctuations in the share price. Share price fluctuations are a result of changes in investors' expectations about earnings growth and dividends. The higher the P/E ratio, the greater the expectations. A low P/E ratio may indicate a bargain or low expectations. There is evidence to suggest that average returns are greater for low P/E shares than for high P/E shares. Higher P/E ratios also tend to occur during periods of low inflation, and lower P/E ratios tend to occur during periods of high inflation.

A P/E ratio in isolation does not tell you very much. It needs to be compared with its average and its range over time. It is also useful to compare it with other firms in the same industry sector and for the overall market. These comparisons will enable you to judge if the share price is at the upper or lower limits of its P/E range and, hence, the upper or lower limits of its value.

P/E ratios for listed shares are reported with the price quotations in *The Australian Financial Review*. P/E ratios for all stocks are affected by changes in the business cycle and emerging trends in the stockmarket. Tracking changes in the All Ordinaries Index P/E ratio is a good way to detect broad changes in market sentiment for equity securities.

Beta factor

A high degree of uncertainty about future returns causes investors to change their minds more frequently, resulting in increased trading and greater price volatility. Statisticians can measure volatility by calculating the *standard deviation* of realised returns. This is an overall measure of investment risk consisting of both systematic risks and specific risks. It is possible, however, to eliminate most of the volatility caused by specific risks. In a portfolio that is perfectly diversified, only the effects of systematic risk remain.

A measure of systematic risk is the *beta factor*, which measures the relative volatility of returns for an individual share compared with the volatility of returns for the overall market. Since capital gains are such a significant part of the rate of return for shares, much of the risk measured by beta is a result of price fluctuations. The market benchmark is based on the All Ordinaries Accumulation Index and is set at 1.0. The beta for an individual share may be greater or less than the market benchmark depending upon its relative volatility.

Shares with a beta greater than 1.0 are more volatile than the market average. They would be expected to gain value faster in a rising market and to lose value faster in a falling market. If a share had a beta of 1.5 and the market return changed by 10 per cent, then the share's return would be expected to change by 15 per cent.

Shares with a beta less than 1.0 are less volatile than the market average. They would be expected to gain value more slowly in a rising market and to lose value more slowly in a falling market. If a share had a beta of 0.5 and the market return changed by 10 per cent, then the share's return would be expected to change by only 5 per cent.

Your stockbroker may be able to provide you with betas for individual shares. There are also information services that provide regularly updated betas. The calculation of beta is not only complex, but it is also plagued by a number of methodological difficulties that weaken its reliability. University academics have been enthusiastically studying betas for a couple of decades; however, many investors have not yet embraced this measure of investment risk.

Large versus small company shares

Another way to think about risk is to consider some of the differences in the risk associated with the shares of small versus large companies.

- Small company shares don't generally trade in large volume, resulting in lack of liquidity in the market, a big spread between the *bid* and *ask* prices, and a tendency towards high price volatility.
- Analysts focus on larger companies, so there is much less research and hence less information available on smaller firms.
- Larger companies have relatively stable earnings derived from a number of different activities, whereas smaller companies tend to focus on only one activity and are more likely to experience greater fluctuations in earnings.
- Smaller firms are generally in need of equity financing which leads to a dilution of earnings per share, whereas larger firms have a greater capacity to raise capital by borrowing—thus leveraging earnings as a result.
- There may be a large shareholder in a smaller company who can artificially drive down the share price if they decide to sell their shares.

Searching for value

One of the keys to searching for value is knowing where to look. Likely hiding places are circumstances that suggest potential for capital gains. Searching for value does not mean acting on the basis of rumours or hot tips. The competition to discover hiding places is intense and there are lots of big game hunters out there looking for the same quarry. The trick is to get in before the circumstances that create value are generally appreciated. Here are some examples.

Cash cows

These are shares with a market price that is below the company's net working capital per share. These companies are loaded with cash and they are particularly attractive because they have the opportunity to make profitable acquisitions or investments. They are also candidates for a merger or takeover offer by others who have good investment opportunities but not the cash to fulfil them. If they also have a large tax loss carry-forward credit, then they are an outstanding candidate.

Thin capitalisation

These are companies with relatively few shares outstanding. The market for their shares is called thin and the share price is generally volatile. Therefore, any positive development is likely to be reflected by a substantial increase in the share price. These shares are also good candidates for a share split if the current price is high.

New floats

Established companies such as Telstra and AMP have been floated on the stock exchange and a number of *initial public offerings* (IPOs) are floated each year. The strong likelihood that a share issue will move towards listing on the ASX is a positive step because it will need to fulfil the ASX listing requirements, implying a certain amount of corporate strength. It will also trade in a market with wider exposure and come under the gaze of more investors. There is evidence that the majority of new floats are under-priced. This all helps to create demand for the shares, resulting in a higher price.

Small company growth

Significant growth potential is usually associated with companies that are young, small and not well-known. Although many large, established companies also possess attractive growth potential, their share price already tends to reflect this condition and they are less likely to have hidden value.

Under-valued assets

Companies carry assets on their books at the price for which they were originally purchased. This is called *book value*. If the asset has increased in value since it was purchased, then its market value may be substantially greater than its book value. If the asset is sold, the company will realise a substantial capital gain on the sale that translates into the share price. Sometimes the market, and even the company itself, may fail to comprehend the value of an asset. Under-valued assets occur most often among oil, mining and other resource shares.

Changes in management or policy

A poor company with good management is a more likely hiding place than a good company with poor management. Changes in management may produce a signal that new developments are likely to occur. The intention of a company to diversify its activities into a promising line of business would represent a potentially favourable policy change.

Hidden earnings

Occasionally the market fails to recognise a turnaround in a company's earnings. Of course, this only persists until the next earnings report is issued. For example, when the price of a commodity rises sharply, such as copper or coal, then those companies producing that commodity experience a substantial increase in earnings. There is a time lag, however, between the increase in the commodity price and a reported increase in the company's earnings.

Buybacks

A buyback consists of a company offering to purchase some of its own ordinary shares. The effect of a buyback is to reduce the number of shares outstanding, thereby increasing the earnings per share for the remaining shares. This should lead to a higher share price. Buybacks are generally the result of a company that has a large cash balance and no developments in which to invest. Some companies buy the shares in small parcels over time; others offer shareholders a premium to the market price.

Technology

Any radical change in technology implies a possibility for hidden value. New products or processes and the impact of high-technology developments in medicine, aerospace, oceanography and computers are good examples.

Legal and political events

Profitable opportunities may arise when a change in the tax law benefits a particular industry or company. Changes in tariffs and other forms of protection from foreign competition may also create the same effect. Shareholders may profit if a court case is resolved in favour of their company. Anything that would markedly boost earnings or increase assets (such as a ruling involving a patent, a valuable mining lease or a reduction in tax liabilities) is in this category.

Takeovers

Most corporate weddings are friendly, with a courtship and a mutual agreement on the merger contract. This permits both companies to calmly work out terms intended to benefit everyone. Sometimes one company decides to acquire another company without bothering to negotiate. A takeover can occur as an off-market offer directly to all shareholders, or it can be an on-market offer to buy shares on the ASX.

A sudden offer for another company's shares with no advance notice is an aggressive act. Investors may view the bidder favourably, but the management of the firm under siege is likely to cry 'raid'. Then the air will be filled with the thunder of charges and counter-charges. If the management of the company that is on the defensive thinks that it may lose control, it may quickly find a merger partner that is more to its liking. The offer price, in cash or securities, is usually well above the current market price because shareholders are unlikely to accept the offer unless they will benefit and the acquiring company won't make an offer unless it sees good value.

Rumours often precede the announcement of merger negotiations, but there is rarely much warning of a surprise takeover bid. Occasionally there is a leak, or a few outsiders are shrewd enough to detect that something is going on, causing an otherwise unexplained rise in the share price. After the announcement, the target company shares will rise to reflect the terms of the offer. If there is any doubt about the deal going through, however, the price won't rise all the way. In a takeover bid for cash, the shares will automatically rise to the bid price if the cash payment is immediately available.

Share splits and bonus issues

Share splits and bonus issues represent additional shares issued by a company to its shareholders for no extra cost. No value is created because the market price automatically adjusts for the increased number of shares outstanding. It is like trading a $10 note for two $5 notes. However, there are more subtle benefits. First, some shareholders actually believe that they have received additional shares for free and regard this as a signal that the company is doing well. Second, if a company cannot afford to pay a cash dividend, it may use a split or a bonus share issue to appease shareholders for the loss of the expected cash dividend. Third, if the dividend per share is maintained after a split or a bonus share issue, then shareholders have effectively received an increase in the dividend.

6

Fundamental analysis

TOP-DOWN APPROACH 75
FINANCIAL STATEMENTS 79
OPERATING PERFORMANCE 86
LIQUIDITY AND SOLVENCY 90
VALUE INDICATORS 92
VALUE VERSUS PRICE 95

The purpose of fundamental analysis is to estimate the *fair value* of a share. It combines the effects of the business cycle, industry sector factors and individual company performance into an estimate of the value for the company's shares. When the fair value of a company's shares has been established, it can be compared to the current market price to decide if the shares would make a good investment.

Top-down approach

Fundamental analysis consists of three layers. The top layer is the overall effect of the economy and the changes that are most likely to occur in the business cycle. The middle layer is the impact of changes in the business cycle upon each of the industry sectors, and other developments that have industry-specific consequences. The bottom layer consists of individual companies and their performance. This is the top-down approach to fundamental analysis.

Riding the business cycle

The Australian economy is characterised by alternating periods of growth and recession that affect the performance of whole industry sectors as well as individual companies. This was described in terms of the *economic clock* in Chapter 2. Expected changes in the business cycle are a major source of fluctuations in share prices. Correctly forecasting changes in the business cycle represents an opportunity to realise capital gains in shares and other securities. Even the professionals, however, have difficulty in accurately forecasting major turning points in the business cycle.

The objective is to anticipate the direction and force of the economic tide so that you will be swimming with the current and not fighting against it. An analysis of the business cycle will not only assist you to decide when to enter or exit the stockmarket, but it will also help you to form a judgement about the impact on individual companies. You need to keep an eye on some of the leading indicators, such as changes in housing starts and home lending, as well as changes in consumer spending. Trying to be a part-time economist, however, usually takes up too much time and effort. For the individual investor, the most effective approach to business cycle analysis is to read the financial press with a view to anticipating where the business cycle is headed.

Examining industry sectors

A company that operates in a dynamic industry has natural advantages over one in a troubled industry. Changes in the business cycle don't affect all industry sectors uniformly. For example, rising interest rates are generally bad news for construction, appliance manufacturers, or industries that produce capital goods. By contrast, industry sectors such as food or health services are not similarly affected. Some industries are directly affected by changes in the business cycle, others are immune to it, and a few industries are counter-cyclical. Many analysts believe that it is more important to be in the right industry sector than in the right stocks. Industry sectors also evolve through successive stages of development. Some sectors take decades to pass through each stage, while others take only a few years. There are four stages of industry development and each represents a different investment environment.

The first stage is a *startup* period in which there are only a few new companies that are developing a new market or product. Most companies are under-financed and incurring operating losses. Their volatile share prices reflect an exciting potential that may or may not be fulfilled. The potential for speculative capital gains is great, but so is the risk.

The second stage is an *expansion* period in which more firms enter the industry and competition increases. There are some spectacular successes and equally spectacular failures during the inevitable shakeout. Takeover activity increases as larger firms consolidate their position in the industry. There is still plenty of potential for capital gains, but investment risk also remains high.

The third stage is a *harvest* period in which the surviving firms are characterised by sufficient capital to continue with expansion, sufficient technology to keep developing new or improved product lines, and sufficient scale to enable low-cost production. This stage may last for a very long time. Most firms in the industry will be earning good profits and paying dividends. There is still potential for moderate capital gains, and investment risk is considerably diminished.

The final stage represents an industry in *stagnation*. It is on the brink of decline unless it can be rejuvenated so that it can continue to harvest. Its competitive advantages have been eroded and, faced with inertia, it is in danger of withering away. Dividend income is generally good because companies are not reinvesting their profits, but there is no longer much potential for capital gains.

Attempting to research everything that affects a particular industry sector can be a difficult and time-consuming task. Most of the large stockbrokers and independent advisory services employ security analysts who specialise in particular industry sectors. Their research reports are generally made available to clients and sometimes you will find extracts published in the financial press.

Evaluating individual companies

Although the companies in a particular industry sector are subject to many of the same influences, they also reflect a great deal of diversity in corporate personality, competitive profile and operating results. The objective is to sift through a promising industry sector in an effort to identify those companies with the best investment potential.

Light-weights are lean, aggressive companies with rapidly increasing sales and profits. They may be riding a wave of industry sector growth, or they may be expanding their market share in a more mature industry. Shares in these companies have volatile prices and pay little or no dividends.

Business cyclists are companies in which sales and earnings expand and contract with the business cycle. Their share price and dividends fluctuate accordingly as they peddle up and down, alternating periods of growth and recession.

Evergreens are large, well-established companies that are not significantly affected by the business cycle. They grow at a steady, moderate rate which is reflected in a moderately increasing share price and dividends.

Heavy-weights are also large, established companies, but growth has either stopped or reversed. They generate more cash flow than they can profitably reinvest, so dividends may indeed be generous. However, the shares don't offer much prospect for capital gains.

Walking wounded are companies that are suffering from a serious injury to their competitive profile. The cause may be damage from new entrants to the industry or from existing competitors, pressure from substitute products and services, price-cutting forced by customers' bargaining power, or increased costs forced by suppliers' bargaining power. Their shares are depressed because of the uncertainty about whether they are going to fail or eventually turn around.

If you want to get behind the public relations hype in order to understand the underlying reasons for a company's performance, then you will need to spend some time and effort getting to know them. You can learn much about individual companies by focusing on the following performance drivers:

- *Management.* Who is the management team? How much experience do they have? Do they have the skills necessary to make this company perform well? How well have they performed in the past? Do they have a well-articulated plan or do they simply react to events?
- *Production.* Is the company a high-cost or low-cost producer? Is it a quality producer? Are earnings substantially influenced by the cost or availability of raw materials? Are wages a significant component of production? Does the company face aggressive trade unions? Does it benefit from technology in the production process? Is there enough capacity to achieve the growth targets?
- *Marketing.* Is the main market industrial, commercial or consumer? Does the company depend on a few large customers or many small ones? Is the product line diversified or specialised? Do the company's products have a good reputation and customer brand loyalty? Is the market large enough to sustain sales growth? How aggressive is the marketing effort and what is the rate of sales growth?
- *Investment.* How is the company improving its product line and productive capacity? How much is spent on research and development? What new products or new applications of existing products are in the pipeline? How much is spent on new plant and equipment, and how will modernisation and expansion improve the company's earning power?
- *Government regulation.* How much does government policy affect earnings? Are sales affected by domestic incentives such as subsidies, or overseas restrictions such as tariffs? To what extent do government agencies dictate how the company may operate and what prices it may charge? How do the government's monetary and fiscal policies affect the company?

Financial statements

An important part of fundamental analysis is the evaluation of company financial statements. It may come as a shock to discover that most of the advisers who make investment recommendations have never actually read the company's financial statements. They generally depend on analysts for this information. Serious investors will learn to read and interpret these statements for themselves.

The three principal financial statements are the statement of financial performance, the statement of financial position and the statement of cash flow. An evaluation of operating performance focuses upon the interrelationships between various items in the financial statements. It enables you to assess the company's efficiency and profitability. An evaluation of liquidity and solvency focuses upon the company's ability to meet its financial obligations. Since it is the company's ordinary shares that are being evaluated, a number of market value indicators are also used.

It is important to keep in mind that audited company financial statements are a statement of opinion, not a statement of fact. Their intent is to present a true and fair picture of the company. However, the application of generally accepted accounting principles is neither consistent nor free from manipulation. For these reasons, great care and judgement are needed in the evaluation of company financial statements.

Statement of financial performance

The statement of financial performance is a company's most important financial statement because it discloses how much the company has earned or lost for its shareholders over a specific period of time. Figure 6.1 is an example of a statement of financial performance.

- The statement of financial performance begins with **operating revenue** and then subtracts the **expenses associated with operations**, leaving **operating profit (or loss) before abnormal items and income tax**.
- You may find some **abnormal items** consisting of items of revenue and expense that are part of the company's normal operations but are abnormal by reason of their size and effect on the operating profit.

Figure 6.1 Statement of financial performance

TYPICAL COMPANY LTD
STATEMENT OF FINANCIAL PERFORMANCE

For the year ending 30 June 2003

		$ million
Operating revenue		480
Operating expenses		
Cost of sales	315	
Interest	5	
Depreciation	10	
Other	80	(410)
Operating profit before abnormal items and income tax		70
Abnormal loss before income tax		(30)
Operating profit before income tax		40
Income tax attributable to operating profit		(16)
Operating profit after income tax		24
Extraordinary items		
Extraordinary loss	(25)	
Less income tax savings	8	(17)
Operating profit and extraordinary items after income tax		7
Retained profits at the beginning of the financial year		61
Total available for appropriation		68
Dividends provided for or paid		(12)
Retained profits at the end of the financial year		56

- This brings us to the **operating profit (or loss) before income tax** from which **income tax attributable to operating profit** is subtracted, leaving the **operating profit (or loss) after income tax**. Operating profit represents the net profit from normal operations attributable to the ordinary shareholders. If there had been any preference shareholders or outside interests, their dividends would have been deducted first.
- You may find some **extraordinary items net of income tax**. These are very rare items of revenue and expense that are

outside the ordinary operations of the company and are not of a recurring nature.

- This brings us to **operating profit and extraordinary items after income tax,** representing the net profit for the period. To this amount is added **retained profits (or accumulated losses) at the beginning of the financial year** and any amounts transferred from reserves, giving us the **total available for appropriation.**
- The total available for appropriation may be used for **dividends, transfers to reserves** and **other appropriations,** or kept in the company as **retained profits (or accumulated losses) at the end of the financial year.** This last amount also appears in the Shareholders' Equity section of the statement of financial position.

Despite the importance of the statement of financial performance, it cannot always be relied upon as an accurate measurement of a company's earnings. Not only is there scope to manipulate reported earnings, but also generally accepted accounting principles are not always applied consistently in determining earnings. Financial analysts refer to *quality of earnings* when they assess the reliability of a company's statement of financial performance. They favour the financial statements of companies with the following characteristics:

- consistent, conservative and prudent accounting policies
- earnings that are stable, predictable and derived from the firm's core operations
- sales that convert quickly into cash
- earnings that are not driven by tax factors or gains from currency or price movements
- a capital structure that has not been manipulated to create earnings

Security analysts may question the quality of reported earnings for companies with one or more of the following warning signals:

- an audit report that is too long, unusually worded or delayed
- the appointment of a new auditor
- changes to less conservative accounting policies
- unusual increases in liability accounts or intangible assets

- non-recurring income such as asset sales
- significant decline in things like research and development, advertising, gross margin, liquid assets or asset turnover
- significant movements in reserves

Statement of financial position

The statement of financial position discloses what the company owns and how it has been financed by its creditors and its shareholders. Figure 6.2 is an example of a statement of financial position.

- The statement of financial position begins with the **assets**, or what the company owns, consisting of **current assets** and **non-current assets**.
- From this are subtracted the **liabilities**, or what the company owes, consisting of **current liabilities** and **non-current liabilities**.
- The difference between the assets and the liabilities is called the **net assets**, which is also equal to shareholders' equity consisting of share capital, reserves, and retained profits or accumulated losses.

The main function of the statement of financial position is to disclose how much the company is worth using generally accepted accounting principles. One of these principles is depreciated or amortised historical cost as the basis for valuing some of the non-current assets. This generally results in a book value for the company that is vastly different from its market value.

A statement of financial position may not actually list all of a company's assets and liabilities. Unless a company expends funds on the purchase or development of an asset, it may not be shown on the statement of financial position. Similarly, increases in asset value as a result of inflation may not be shown. Sometimes these hidden assets represent a significant contribution to a company's worth. Moreover, it is not easy for a company to know what liabilities may occur in the future or to quantify them accurately. Look for references to potential future liabilities in other parts of the annual report such as the footnotes.

Figure 6.2 Statement of financial position

TYPICAL COMPANY LTD
STATEMENT OF FINANCIAL POSITION

As at 30 June 2003

		$ million
ASSETS		
Current		
Cash	6	
Receivables	24	
Inventories	30	60
Non-current		
Investments	30	
Property, plant and equipment	50	
Intangibles	20	100
Total assets		160
LIABILITIES		
Current		
Creditors and borrowings	10	
Provision for income tax	8	
Provision for dividend	12	30
Non-current		
Creditors and borrowings		34
Total liabilities		64
NET ASSETS		96
SHAREHOLDERS' EQUITY		
Ordinary shares	40	
Retained profits	56	96

Statement of cash flow

The statement of cash flow complements the statement of financial position and the statement of financial performance. It is a reconciliation of the opening and closing cash balance in the statement of financial position and it can be used to assess the ability of the company to generate cash flow, meet its financial commitments, fund its activities and obtain external finance. It is more reliable than the statement of financial performance because it is subject to less manipulation. Figure 6.3 is an example.

- Cash flow from *operating activities* is generally the main source of cash flow. It consists of receipts from customers, payments to suppliers, salaries and wages, interest payments and taxes. It also includes any changes in net working capital.
- Cash flow from *investing activities* includes the purchase and/or sale of non-current assets. It is not unusual for a company to have negative cash flow from investing activities related to the acquisition of long-term assets.
- Cash flow from *financing activities* includes borrowing and repayment, share issues and buybacks, and dividends.
- The statement of cash flow is a good check on the statement of financial performance. It is possible for the statement of

Figure 6.3 Statement of cash flow

TYPICAL COMPANY LTD
STATEMENT OF CASH FLOW

For the year ending 30 June 2003

		$ million
Cash flow from operating activities		
Receipts from customers	480	
Payments to suppliers	(300)	
Salaries and wages paid	(150)	
Interest paid	(5)	
Taxes paid	(15)	10
Cash flow from investing activities		
Payments for property, plant and equipment	(50)	(50)
Cash flow from financing activities		
Proceeds from borrowing	34	
Dividends paid	(12)	22
Net increase (decrease) in cash		(18)
Cash ceginning of the year		24
Cash end of the year		6

financial performance to show a profit when cash flow is negative. If the cash flowing into a company exceeds the cash flowing out, then it can continue to operate regardless of its profitability. However, if the cash flowing out of a company repeatedly exceeds the cash flowing in, then eventually the company will run out of cash and grind to a halt. Profits are not cash, and that is why the statement of cash flow is a valuable check on the other financial reports.

Operating performance

The most widely practised method of analysing and interpreting financial statements is by the use of ratios. Financial ratios in isolation, however, have little significance. What we need to make judgements about good or bad financial ratios is something with which to compare them. There are three ways to make comparisons. Comparisons with past financial ratios tell us whether the trends are getting better or worse. Comparisons with the financial ratios of similar firms or industry averages tell us how well a company stacks up against the performance of other companies in the same line of business. Comparisons with rule-of-thumb standards tell us how a company compares with commonly accepted benchmarks.

An analysis of operating performance focuses upon profitability, efficiency and the effects of financial leverage. It consists of finding answers to a number of questions. How profitable is each dollar of sales? How efficiently do the assets generate sales? How do profitability and efficiency combine to produce a return on the investment in assets? What proportion of the assets has been funded by the shareholders? How much does borrowing leverage the return on assets into a return for the shareholders?

Operating profit margin

This ratio represents the average operating profit per dollar of operating revenue. Extraordinary items are not included because they would distort the analysis of operating performance.

$$\text{Operating profit margin} = \frac{\text{Operating profit after tax}}{\text{Operating revenue}} = \frac{\$24\ 000\ 000}{\$480\ 000\ 000} = 5\%$$

Operating profit margin can vary significantly from one type of business to another and should always be assessed together with asset turnover. We are looking for an operating margin that not only compares favourably with other firms in the same industry sector, but also improves over time.

Asset turnover

Asset turnover measures how hard the company's total asset base is working to generate sales.

$$\text{Asset turnover} = \frac{\text{Operating revenue}}{\text{Total assets}} = \frac{\$480\ 000\ 000}{\$160\ 000\ 000} = 3 \text{ times}$$

Greater asset turnover indicates more efficient use of assets to generate sales, and less asset turnover indicates less efficient use of assets to generate sales. The rate of asset turnover varies significantly from one industry sector to another, so we are looking for companies that compare favourably with other companies in the same industry sector.

Return on assets

This ratio is used to assess the profit-earning performance of the company's assets. It relates the operating profit after tax to the investment in assets. We are looking for a return on assets that not only compares favourably with other firms in the same industry sector, but also improves over time.

$$\text{Return on assets} = \frac{\text{Operating profit after tax}}{\text{Total assets}} = \frac{\$24\ 000\ 000}{\$160\ 000\ 000} = 15\%$$

Return on assets is affected by the combined performance of operating profit margin and asset turnover. Return on assets can also be found by multiplying operating profit margin by asset turnover.

Return on assets = Operating profit margin x Asset turnover = 5% x 3 = 15%

Return on assets links the dynamic relationship between operating revenue, costs and profits with the underlying asset base. A decline in the return on assets will occur if sales fall or expenses rise faster than sales. A decline can also occur if the investment in assets increases at a faster rate than operating profit after tax.

Shareholders' interest

Most companies make use of borrowed capital. Borrowing not only makes it possible to leverage the shareholders' equity, but also enables the company to finance opportunities that would otherwise have to be forgone. The proportions of debt and equity capital in financing the company's assets are usually referred to as *financial structure*. One way of looking at financial structure is to focus on the proportion of total assets represented by the shareholders' equity. We call this *shareholders' interest*.

$$\text{Shareholders' interest} = \frac{\text{Shareholders' equity}}{\text{Total assets}} = \frac{\$96\ 000\ 000}{\$160\ 000\ 000} = 60\%$$

If shareholders have financed 60 per cent of the company's assets, then creditors have financed the remaining 40 per cent. An important and difficult question for both management and investors is how much debt is too much debt. The acceptable proportion of debt varies among different industry sectors. Debt finance can enable a company to grow and to improve its profitability, but too much debt exposes it to the risk of financial loss and potential insolvency.

Return on shareholders' equity

This ratio is one of the best indicators of overall performance. It reflects the earning power of the shareholders' investment in the company. It can be compared with the return from any alternative investment. If there were no liabilities, the return on shareholders' equity would be the same as the return on assets. However, return on shareholders' equity is amplified by the extent to which the company has borrowed or leveraged its equity.

$$\text{Return on shareholders' equity} = \frac{\text{Operating profit after tax}}{\text{Shareholders' equity}} = \frac{\$24\ 000\ 000}{\$96\ 000\ 000} = 25\%$$

Return on shareholders' equity can also be found by dividing return on assets by shareholders' interest. These underlying ratios can be used to explain changes in the return on shareholders' equity.

$$\text{Return on shareholders' equity} = \frac{\text{Return on assets}}{\text{Shareholders' interest}} = \frac{0.15}{0.60} = 25\%$$

Operating performance model

The operating performance model represents a framework for organising the analysis of these ratios. It is a powerful tool that can be used to identify important variables in a company's financial statements, determine the cause and effect between those variables, and direct your attention towards changes that may affect the value of the company's securities. Figure 6.4 represents the operating performance model.

Figure 6.4 Operating performance model

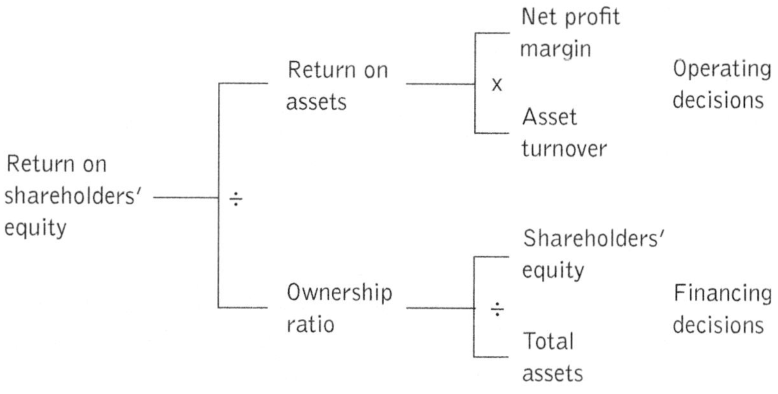

The objective is to maximise return on shareholders' equity. It is composed of two underlying factors—return on assets and shareholders' interest. Return on assets is an overall measure of how well the company's asset base produces a profit. It reflects *operating decisions* over buying, selling, expense control and asset management. Shareholders' interest is a measure of the shareholders' investment in the company's asset base. It reflects *financing decisions* over how much capital has been borrowed and the degree to which the company has leveraged its financial structure.

Liquidity and solvency

Liquidity ratios reflect the ability of a company to meet its current financial commitments. *Solvency* ratios take a longer view and are particularly important to holders of the company's fixed interest securities. Inability to satisfy the legitimate demands of creditors is sufficient reason for a company to be wound up. These ratios, therefore, are mostly concerned with the financial health of the company and its 'survivability'. They should be evaluated in conjunction with the statement of cash flow.

Current ratio

The current ratio is the most commonly used test of liquidity since it indicates the extent to which the claims of short-term creditors are covered by assets that can be quickly converted into cash.

$$\text{Current ratio} = \frac{\text{Current assets}}{\text{Current liabilities}} = \frac{\$60\ 000\ 000}{\$30\ 000\ 000} = 2$$

A current ratio of 2 to 1 means that current assets equal twice the current liabilities, and the generally accepted rule of thumb is that the current ratio should be about 2 to 1 or better. If a company has growing sales and a short cash cycle, however, then a lower current ratio can be quite satisfactory.

Liquid ratio or acid test

Creditors often question the liquidity of a company's inventory. They reason that since inventory is two steps away from cash, it should not be considered available to pay bills that are immediately due. They prefer to use the liquid ratio or acid test in which inventory is subtracted from the current assets.

$$\text{Liquid ratio} = \frac{\text{Current assets} - \text{Inventory}}{\text{Current liabilities}} = \frac{\$60\ 000\ 000 - \$30\ 000\ 000}{\$30\ 000\ 000} = 1$$

The rule of thumb for the liquid ratio is 1 to 1. While it needs to be interpreted with the same care as the current ratio, significant deviations below 1 to 1 are usually viewed with concern.

Net working capital to sales

A company needs to maintain enough working capital to adequately service its sales volume. If net working capital declines relative to sales, there may be an impending liquidity problem. Net working capital is the difference between current assets and current liabilities.

$$\text{Net working capital to sales} = \frac{\text{Current assets} - \text{Current liabilities}}{\text{Operating revenue}}$$

$$\frac{\$60\ 000\ 000 - \$30\ 000\ 000}{\$480\ 000\ 000} = 0.0625$$

In this example, net working capital to sales may be a bit low at 6.25 cents per dollar of sales. Although the current ratio and quick ratio are normal, the net working capital to sales ratio would tell us to keep an eye on the company's liquidity. If the ratio is trending downward, our concern would be greater.

Interest cover

The interest cover ratio measures the extent to which earnings are available to pay the fixed interest charges. Failure to meet this obligation usually results in legal action by creditors. The ratio is found by dividing Earnings Before Interest and Taxes (EBIT) by the amount of the fixed interest charges. EBIT is found by adding the interest charges back to operating profit before income tax. The interest cover ratio in this example is comfortable because there is enough EBIT to pay the interest nine times.

$$\text{Interest cover} = \frac{\text{EBIT}}{\text{Interest}} = \frac{\$45\ 000\ 000}{\$5\ 000\ 000} = 9 \text{ times}$$

Debt to equity ratio

The debt to equity ratio is another way of looking at capital structure. It is used to measure the amount of long-term borrowing compared with shareholders' equity. The lower the debt to equity ratio, the less likelihood of insolvency. Debt to equity ratios vary substantially and should be compared with the average for the industry sector.

$$\text{Debt to equity ratio} = \frac{\text{Non-current liabilities}}{\text{Shareholders' equity}} = \frac{\$34\ 000\ 000}{\$96\ 000\ 000} = 35.4\%$$

Value indicators

Value indicators relate the information in the company's financial statements to the company's ordinary shares. Let us assume that the price of Typical Company Ltd shares is $8. This is the value that the market has placed on the company's shares based on current and expected dividends, earnings and asset backing. A very important part of the analysis of equity securities is to evaluate the market value in terms of the information disclosed in the company financial reports. Most of this information is reported in the financial press along with the share price quotations.

Dividend payout

The dividend payout is the proportion of annual operating profit after tax that is paid out in dividends to the ordinary shareholders.

It reflects the dividend policy of the company that results in income to shareholders.

$$\text{Dividend payout} = \frac{\text{Dividends provided for or paid}}{\text{Operating profit after tax}} = \frac{\$12\ 000\ 000}{\$24\ 000\ 000} = 50\%$$

Dividend per share (DPS)

This is the amount of dividends provided for or paid in the past year divided by the average number of ordinary shares outstanding.

$$\text{Dividend per share} = \frac{\text{Dividends provided for or paid}}{\text{Ordinary shares outstanding}} = \frac{\$12\ 000\ 000}{30\ 000\ 000} = \$0.40$$

Dividend yield

The dividend yield reflects the income-producing capacity of a share based on the annual DPS and the current share price.

$$\text{Dividend yield} = \frac{\text{Dividends per share}}{\text{Share price}} = \frac{\$0.40}{\$8.00} = 5\%$$

Earnings per share (EPS)

Investors are more interested in earnings per share than in total earnings. EPS can be found by dividing annual operating profit after tax by the number of ordinary shares outstanding. EPS is not only affected by changes in profitability, but also by changes in the number of shares outstanding.

$$\text{Earnings per share} = \frac{\text{Operating profit after tax}}{\text{Ordinary shares outstanding}} = \frac{\$24\ 000\ 000}{30\ 000\ 000} = \$0.80$$

EPS growth rate

The EPS growth rate measures how much per share earnings are capable of growing without further outside financing. It can be estimated by multiplying the return on shareholders' equity by the retention rate. The retention rate is equal to 100 per cent minus the dividend payout. Using the information for Typical Company Ltd, the EPS growth rate is 12.5 per cent.

$$\text{EPS growth rate} = \text{Return on equity} \times (100\% - \text{Dividend payout})$$
$$= 25\% \times (100\% - 50\%) = 12.5\%$$

The estimate of current earnings growth is important, but what really matters is any change that may be expected to occur in the future. If you expect the growth rate to be different in the future, then you should be using the expected growth rate. The operating performance model provides an excellent framework for anticipating changes in return on shareholders' equity which is the key to future changes in the EPS growth rate.

Price–earnings ratio

The P/E ratio expresses the current share price as a multiple of the most recent annual earnings per share.

$$\text{P/E ratio} = \frac{\text{Share price}}{\text{Earnings per share}} = \frac{\$8.00}{\$0.80} = 10 \text{ times}$$

As a general rule, the P/E ratio is a means of measuring investors' expectations of future performance. A low P/E ratio is an indication that investors are not optimistic about future performance. A high P/E ratio generally indicates investor optimism about future performance.

Price–earnings growth ratio (PEG ratio)

The PEG is the ratio of the P/E ratio to the earnings per share growth rate.

$$\text{PEG ratio} = \frac{\text{P/E ratio}}{\text{EPS growth rate}} = \frac{10 \text{ times}}{12.5\%} = 0.8$$

In general, the P/E ratio should equal the long-term earnings per share growth rate, so a ratio of 1.0 is considered to represent fair value. A PEG that is less than 1.0 means that the share is under-priced relative to fair value, and a PEG that is more than 1.0 means that the share is over-priced relative to fair value.

Net asset backing (NAB)

Net asset backing per share tells us what each ordinary share would be worth if all of the assets were sold at their statement of financial position values and all of the debts were repaid. NAB excludes intangible assets on the conservative premise that they may have no realisable value.

$$\text{Net asset backing} = \frac{\text{Assets} - \text{Liabilities} - \text{Intangibles}}{\text{Ordinary shares outstanding}}$$

$$\frac{\$160\ 000\ 000 - \$64\ 000\ 000 - \$20\ 000\ 000}{30\ 000\ 000} = \$2.53$$

The price to NAB ratio reflects the relationship between the share price and net tangible assets per share. A company with strong management that has learned to function efficiently and profitably should have a price to NAB ratio that is significantly greater than 1.0.

$$\text{Price to NAB} = \frac{\text{Current share price}}{\text{Net tangible assets per share}} = \frac{\$8.00}{\$2.53} = 3.16 \text{ times}$$

Value versus price

Price and value are not the same thing. If the fair value of a share is significantly greater than its market price, then you may want to buy it in anticipation of a capital gain. If fair value is less than market price, then you may want to sell any shares that you own.

For years, the academic community has been trying to convince itself and investors that the stockmarket prices shares *efficiently*, the implication being that a share's price is a true reflection of its fair value and that it is fruitless to look for shares that are mispriced. However, share prices do diverge from their fair value and there are plenty of historical examples to illustrate the point. In practice, establishing the fair value of a share is more of an art than a precise science. It has a great deal more to do with making judgements about things that may happen in the future than it does with merely analysing current facts. The ability to foresee likely future events and their effect on a company's share price is the key element in successfully searching for value.

There are a number of established methods for estimating the fair value of a share. We shall focus on two approaches that are appropriate for the shares of publicly listed companies. They are the *earnings approach* and the *present value approach*. Both approaches need to be applied with judgement, however, because they are very sensitive to variations in the input variables.

Earnings approach

The earnings approach is suitable for valuing shares in companies with stable earnings per share. It requires two input variables. The first is an estimate of the most likely EPS that the company can be expected to achieve during the holding period. The second is an estimate of the most likely P/E ratio that the market will place on the company's shares.

Typical Company Ltd has an EPS of 80 cents. The historical EPS growth rate has been 12.5 per cent per year. Therefore, if things continue as before, then the expected EPS for next year will be ($0.80 × 1.125) = 90 cents. Typical Company Ltd has a current market price of $8 per share and a current P/E ratio of 10 times. The most important influences on the future P/E ratio are the firm's dividend policy, the rate of growth in EPS and the degree of certainty about expected future earnings. Fair value using the earnings approach consists of multiplying the expected EPS by the expected P/E ratio. The estimate of fair value for Typical Company Ltd shares is $9. It exceeds the market price of $8 by $1, representing a potential capital gain.

Fair value = Expected EPS x Expected P/E ratio = $0.90 x 10 = $9.00

Present value approach

Fair value based on the present value approach is more appropriate when the EPS pattern is not stable. It is also valuable as a cross-check on the earnings approach. It consists of finding the *present value* of expected future dividends and the expected future resale price of the shares.

The present value approach incorporates the share's beta. It is part of the *Capital Asset Pricing Model*, which provides us with a discount rate to use in the present value calculation. The Capital Asset Pricing Model says that the required rate of return for a share consists of the *risk-free rate of return* plus a *risk premium*.

The risk-free rate of return is usually regarded as the yield on a Commonwealth treasury note. The risk premium depends upon the share's beta and the difference between the expected return for the overall market and the risk-free rate of return. Typical Company Ltd shares have a beta of 1.5 times, the risk-free rate of return on a short-term Commonwealth treasury note is 7 per cent, and the expected market return is 13 per cent. Therefore, the risk premium is 9 per cent.

Risk premium = Beta x (Expected market return – Risk-free rate)
= 1.5 x (13% – 7%) = 9%

Adding the risk-free rate of return and the risk premium together gives us a required rate of return of 16 per cent. This is the required rate of return that we use to find the present value of Typical Company Ltd shares.

Required rate of return = Risk-free rate of return + Risk premium
= 7% + 9% = 16%

Figure 6.5 illustrates a forecast for the expected dividends and share price over a three-year holding period. Typical Company Ltd is expected to have an EPS growth rate of 50 per cent in Year 1 and to remain flat in Years 2 and 3. The payout ratio is expected to remain at 50 per cent of EPS, resulting in the forecast for dividends. If the expected P/E ratio is 10 times, then the forecast share price at the end of Year 3 will be $12.

Figure 6.5 Present value

	Current year actual	Year 1 forecast	Year 2 forecast	Year 3 forecast
EPS growth rate	12.5%	50%	nil	nil
EPS	$0.80	$1.20	$1.20	$1.20
Payout	50%	50%	50%	50%
Dividends	$0.40	$0.60	$0.60	$0.60
P/E ratio	10 times			10 times
Share price	$8.00			$12.00

The required rate of return is used as a discount rate to find the present value of the expected dividends and the expected resale price. The estimate of fair value is about $9. It exceeds the current market price of $8 by $1, representing a potential gain.

$$\text{Fair value} = \frac{\$0.60}{1.16} + \frac{\$0.60}{(1.16)^2} + \frac{\$0.60 + \$12.00}{(1.16)^3} \approx \$9.00$$

7

Technical analysis

TECHNICAL TRADING SYSTEMS 100
MARKET INDICATORS 102
CHARTING TECHNIQUES 103
ARTIFICIAL INTELLIGENCE 112
AUSTRALIAN SOFTWARE SUPPLIERS 113
AUSTRALIAN DATA SUPPLIERS 116

So far we have been concentrating on *fundamental analysis* which endeavours to determine a share's fair value. This chapter focuses on a different approach called *technical analysis* in which the emphasis is on information generated by the market itself. Technical analysis is the study of supply and demand factors that influence the prices of securities. It uses information about past prices and trading volume to predict future price trends.

Most finance academics take the view that technical analysis has little or no forecasting ability. However, a lot of professional investors regularly use technical analysis, and this suggests that they derive some benefit from it. Moreover, technical analysts have developed many new and sophisticated trading systems that academics have not subjected to detailed statistical analysis. At the very least, every investor should know enough about technical analysis to understand the recommendations based on this approach and to evaluate the comments that appear daily in the financial press.

The purpose of this chapter is to survey some of the established technical trading systems, introduce some new ones, and identify sources of software and data. The chapter begins with an explanation of the thinking behind technical trading systems. Then it goes on to describe market indicators, charting methods, and two artificial intelligence techniques called neural networks and genetic algorithms. The last two sections list sources of technical trading software and data suppliers.

Technical trading systems

The forerunner of technical analysis is the Dow theory. It was conceived by Charles Dow who edited the *Wall Street Journal* from 1889 to 1902. The Dow theory can be explained by analogy. Suppose you are on the beach and you want to know if the tide is coming in or going out. In the short run, it is not easy to be sure because of the fluctuating waves and ripples that obscure the main tidal action. However, if you place a stake in the sand at the highest point of each wave, you will soon be able to detect if the tide is rising or falling. Dow's concept of the stockmarket was that it was composed of major trends analogous to the tides, intermediate trends analogous to waves, and minor trends analogous to ripples.

Investors who rely on technical trading systems hold the view that all of the fundamentals are already built into price. Therefore, they concentrate on identifying a trend at an early stage in order to take a position that profits from it. There are a number of underlying assumptions that underpin technical trading systems.

- The market value of every security is determined by the interaction of supply and demand for that security.
- Supply and demand are governed by both rational and irrational investor behaviour.
- Market prices tend to move in trends that last for some time.
- Changes in trends are the result of shifting supply and demand that can be detected in the patterns of the market prices themselves.

Technical analysis uses a specialised language. A strong upward price trend is called a *bull market*. A strong downward price trend is called a *bear market*. When no trend is apparent, the market is described as going *sideways*. If the price drops briefly during a bull market, it is called a *correction* or a *reaction*. If the price rises briefly in a bear market, it is called a *rally*. When the price levels off, it is variously referred to as a *consolidation*, *congestion* or *building a base*. Buy and sell signals are based upon evidence of *accumulation* (buying) or *distribution* (selling).

The foundation of technical analysis is *support* and *resistance* levels. A support level is a price at which a substantial surge in demand is expected because heavy buying has typically occurred around this price in the past. A resistance level is a price at which a substantial surge in supply is expected because heavy selling has typically occurred around this price in the past. Prices tend to *bottom out* at support levels and *top out* at resistance levels. Any price movement that breaks through these levels is a strong indication that a new trend has developed.

The reasoning behind support and resistance levels is really quite simple. If investors have bought at a given price and then watched a decline in price, the natural human tendency is to wait until they get even and then sell. This creates a resistance level to any subsequent upward movement. Conversely, if investors see a price rise, then they will probably be eager to buy if the price falls back to the old level again. This creates a support level for any subsequent downward movement.

There are many forms of technical analysis. Some are concerned with simply identifying the direction of a trend. Some try to establish the strength or momentum of a trend. Others attempt to forecast an impending reversal in a trend. Technical analysis focuses the mind on what the market is actually doing, rather than on what the fundamentals say it should be doing.

Technical analysis is gaining a new popularity in Australia. The Securities Institute of Australia runs a diploma of technical analysis, and the Australian Technical Analysts Association (ATAA) runs a more informal education program. The ATAA has been in operation for over ten years and is affiliated with the International Federation of Technical Analysts. It has branches in all Australian capital cities and you can contact them by visiting their Internet site at http://www.ataa.com.au.

Market indicators

In Australia, the performance of the stockmarket is generally measured in terms of the All Ordinaries Index. Market indicators are commonly used to judge the strength of a market trend once it is under way. Three popular market indicators are the advance–decline line, the high–low index and the pattern of trading volume.

Advance–decline line

The advance–decline line can be used to assess the breadth of buying or selling pressure across the stockmarket. It consists of the number of rising shares minus the number of falling shares each day. This information is reported in the financial press. The result of each day's advance–decline calculation is added to a cumulative total that is plotted on a chart along with the All Ordinaries Index.

Because the All Ordinaries Index is value-weighted, it is heavily influenced by trading in the shares of the largest companies. This results in the possibility that the index can go in one direction when the majority of the smaller company shares have actually gone in the opposite direction. Such a divergence between the index and the listed shares of smaller companies means that many stocks may not be participating in the market movement.

The advance–decline line measures whether the market is gaining or losing strength. If it follows the trend in the All Ordinaries Index, then it is a confirmation of the trend. If the All Ordinaries Index is rising and the advance–decline line falls, however, it suggests that the rising market is running out of steam. Similarly, if the All Ordinaries Index is falling and the advance–decline line begins to rise, it suggests that selling pressure is easing relative to buying pressure.

High–low index

Another measure that can be used to supplement or confirm the advance–decline line is the high–low index. A rising stockmarket will be characterised by an increasing number of shares that are reaching new highs for the year and a decreasing number of shares that are experiencing new lows for the year. The opposite occurs in a falling market. This information is also reported in the financial press.

The number of ASX shares reaching new highs for the year minus the number of shares making new lows for the year is averaged for some period such as five days. The moving average smooths out erratic daily fluctuations. The high–low index generally moves in the same direction as the market. Divergence from the market trend is a clue to a trend reversal and it can be used to confirm a similar signal from the advance–decline line.

Trading volume

Technical analysts maintain that you cannot forecast the market strictly on the basis of price. Trading volume, or the number of shares traded, is equally important because it tells us something about the strength of a change in the All Ordinaries Index. A popular rule in technical trading systems is that volume goes with the trend. This means that in a bull market, trading volume is supposed to be strong when prices are rising and weak on reactions. In a bear market, trading volume is supposed to be strong when prices are falling and weak on rallies. Bull market peaks and bear market troughs are often characterised by diminishing volume heralding the reversal of a trend.

Charting techniques

Technical analysis is an attempt to forecast future prices by studying past prices. Traditionally, this has been done using various types of charts that provide a visual record of past prices. A chart can record prices for shares, options, futures contracts, an industry average or the All Ordinaries Index. The purpose of recording prices is to establish the high and low points of past investor enthusiasm with a view to anticipating future price movements.

It is easy enough to record share prices and trading volume, but interpreting charts correctly is more of an art than a science. Technical analysts often disagree about what a chart is telling them. False signals, whipsaws and other errors are inevitable. Despite the shortcomings of charting, many investors use this form of technical analysis and a number of charting services are offered by subscription. There are four conventional types of charts—the bar chart, the candlestick chart, the point and figure chart, and moving averages.

Bar chart

Perhaps the most widely used form of charting is the high–low-close bar chart. Figure 7.1 is an example of a bar chart. On the vertical axis is the price scale. Each vertical line, or bar, connects the highest and lowest price during trading. The closing price is indicated by a cross hatch on the bar. The horizontal axis at the bottom of the chart records the time scale. The vertical lines at the bottom of the chart record the number of shares traded. Most bar charts are recorded daily, but longer-term charts are sometimes done on a weekly or monthly basis.

The key to charting is interpretation. Technical analysts look for price and volume patterns that tell them what the price is likely to do next. An important assumption in technical analysis is that once a trend is established, it will persist for some time. The obvious corollary is that breaking a trend is a significant event.

A bar chart provides a visual record of a price trend. Bull market trends tend to be slow and take some time to develop. A bullish chart pattern may be a decisive upside breakout from a previously established trading range or a price that is holding above a previously established support level. Bear market trends tend to be faster and take less time to develop. A bearish chart pattern may be a decisive downside breakout from a previously established trading range or a price that is falling away from a previously established resistance level.

Heavy trading volume is interpreted as strength in the underlying trend. Light trading volume is interpreted as weakness in

Figure 7.1 Daily bar chart

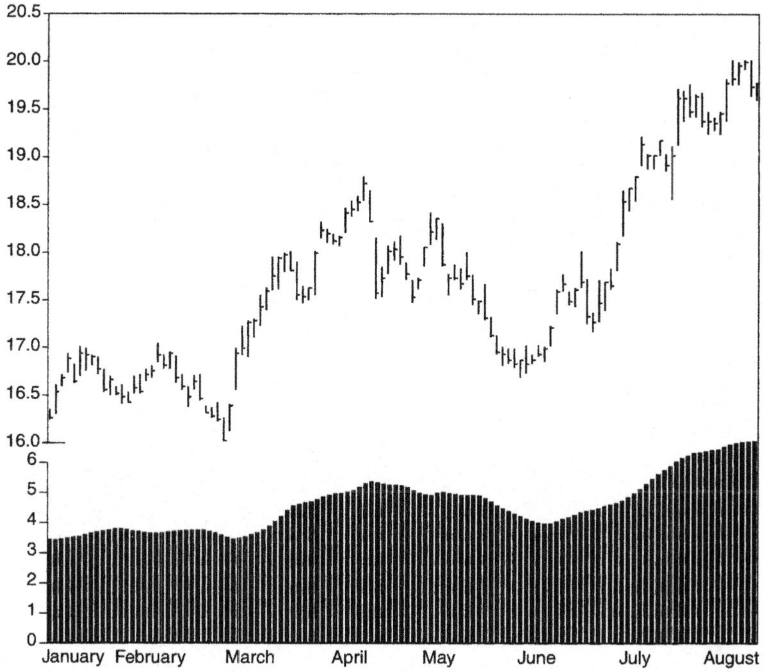

the underlying trend. A rising price on increasing volume is an indication of a continuing up-trend, while a falling price on increasing volume is an indication of a continuing down-trend. A rising price on light volume is an indication that the up-trend is weak, and a falling price on light volume is an indication that the down-trend may soon reverse.

The bar chart in Figure 7.1 begins with a period of consolidation on light volume between a support level at \$16 and a resistance level at \$17. There is a strong upside breakout through the \$17 resistance level on rising volume signalling an upward trend. The price reaches \$18.50 before a correction back to \$17 on decreasing volume. Then the trend resumes with a strong recovery on heavy volume to reach \$20. The record of past prices is clear. The technical analyst's challenge is to predict what will happen next.

Candlestick chart

The candlestick charting system uses the open, high, low and closing prices in a way that is similar to the bar chart. The difference is that the bar is now a candlestick. The candlestick is filled in when the closing price is below the opening price, and it is left open when the closing price is above the opening price. The candlesticks help to identify strength and weakness. Figure 7.2 is the candlestick version of the bar chart in Figure 7.1.

Figure 7.2 Candlestick chart

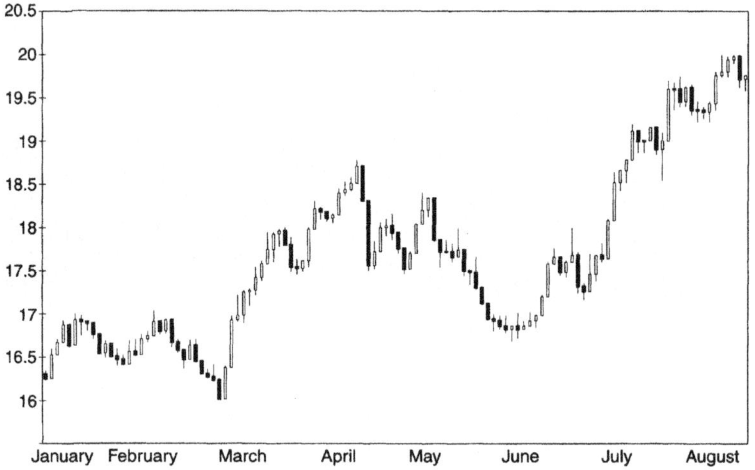

Point and figure chart

The proponents of point and figure charts contend that market prices spend the majority of the time going sideways. The point and figure chart condenses the sideways movements and focuses more clearly on the important rises and falls. Consequently, support and resistance patterns are easier to identify and important buy and sell signals are easier to recognise.

Point and figure charts do this by dispensing with the time axis. In this way, they capture each significant price movement regardless of how long it takes to occur. These charts also ignore trading volume. According to point and figure chartists, when the price breaks out of a horizontal trading range, it will continue vertically for the same distance that it went across. This process of determining the extent of a rise or a fall is known as the *count*. Figure 7.3 is the point and figure equivalent of the previous examples.

There are two elements that need to be selected for a point and figure chart. The first element is the scale on the vertical price axis which is known as the *box size*. The box size is usually smaller for short-term trading and larger for longer-term trading. In Figure 7.3, the box size is 20 cents. The second element is the *reversal size*. This is the number of boxes that the price must reverse before we begin a new column. In Figure 7.3, the reversal size is one box. The conventional symbols are **X** in rising columns and **O** in falling columns. *Course of sales* price data are ideal for point and figure charting.

Figure 7.3 Point and figure chart

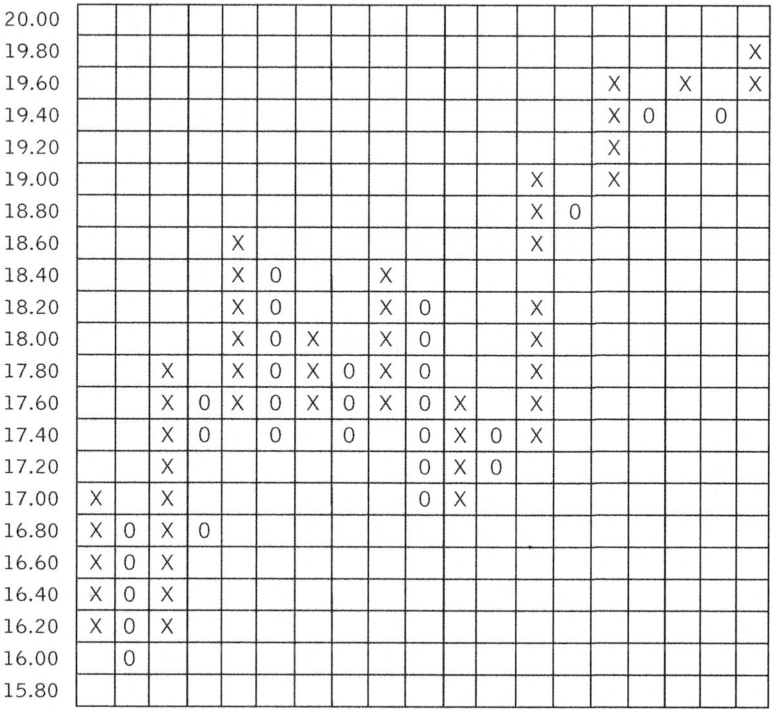

Elliott wave theory

The Elliott wave theory holds that market behaviour is predictable because mass investor psychology swings from pessimism to optimism and back in a natural sequence. This sequence creates specific patterns in price movement. The most important principle of the Elliott wave theory is that major price moves take place in five waves. In a major bull market, the first wave is upward, the second is a downward correction, the third wave is upward, the fourth wave is a downward correction and the fifth wave is upward again. According to the theory, the first, third and fifth upward waves can be further subdivided into five wave patterns. The second and fourth waves, however, are subdivided differently into three waves because they are in the opposite direction to the main trend.

The Elliott wave theory is interwoven with *Fibonacci numbers*. These numbers consist of a series in which each number is the sum of the two before it—0, 1, 1, 2, 3, 5, 8, 13, 21, 34 and so on. As the sequence progresses, the ratio between each number and its predecessor tends towards the value of 1.618 which has been known throughout history as the golden mean. Knowing where to look for the Fibonacci relationship is the key to its application to the Elliott wave theory.

The Elliott wave theory is an interesting tool for giving broad historical perspective to market movements. Some difficulties occur when it is used in an attempt to recognise intermediate and minor waves. Nevertheless, it has proven to be effective as a trend identification device.

Gann analysis

The Gann system is a collection of several techniques that are tied together by the assumption of underlying and predictable cycles in price and time. Its unique contribution is to treat time and price as one dimension rather than two. Support and resistance, for example, occur in time as well as in price. Gann analysis consists of four main elements:

- *Angles*—key angles from the horizontal on a Gann chart define support and resistance levels.
- *Anniversary dates*—key intervals of time in which important events are likely to be repeated.
- *Cardinal squares*—a square on a Gann chart that is composed of numbers spiralling progressively outward from the lowest all-time price. Key angles drawn from the centre of the square identify significant support and resistance levels.
- *Price–time squares*—a square on a Gann chart that is derived from the high and low prices for a period. Diagonals and other significant lines on the square define Gann angles.

Anniversary dates are used to predict price reversals. Cardinal squares are used to predict the level at which a price or time reversal will take place. Price–time squares provide the framework for the angles. Percentage retracements can be calculated using Fibonacci numbers. Gann charts require a greater commitment of time and effort than most other technical trading systems; however, there are commercial software packages, newsletters and other services for Gann devotees.

Moving averages

A moving average of past prices can be used as an indicator of a price trend. A *simple moving average* is calculated by adding together the closing prices during the averaging period and dividing by the number of trading days. An alternative to the simple moving average is the *weighted moving average* in which recent prices are given greater weight so that the moving average will be more representative of the current market trend. Some chartists prefer the *exponential moving average* because it produces a smoother line. All of these calculations can be handled easily by a spreadsheet package on your personal computer. Figure 7.4 is an example of two moving averages superimposed over the bar chart from Figure 7.1. The thick line is a 35-day moving average and the thin line is a ten-day moving average.

Finding the right number of days to use in the averaging period is important. Long-term investors often use a 200-day

Figure 7.4 Moving averages

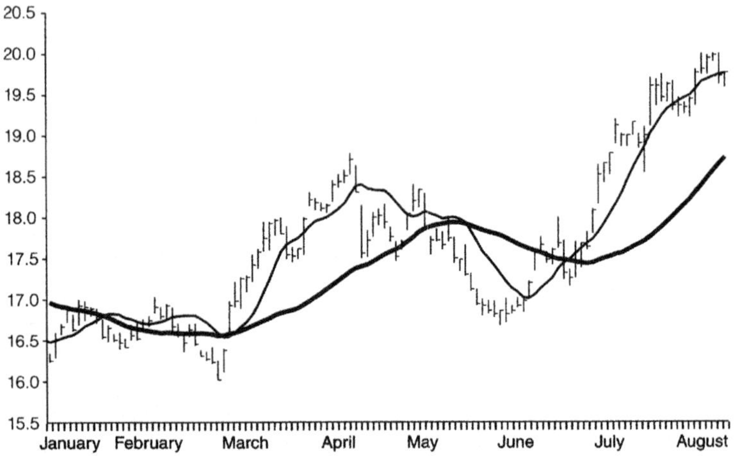

moving average, whereas short-term investors may prefer a five-day moving average. Since it is a cumulative indicator, the longer the averaging period, the more sluggish the moving average will be. If you want a more sensitive moving average, make it shorter. However, a very short moving average can be too sensitive, causing it to *whipsaw* resulting in a large number of false signals. There are two main trading rules for moving averages:

- A buy signal is given when the price moves up and crosses over the moving average from below.
- A sell signal is given when the price moves down and crosses over the moving average from above.

The *Moving Average Convergence Divergence* indicator (MACD) is another way to use moving averages. It is a way of comparing the short-term trend with the long-term trend by plotting a long-term moving average together with a short-term moving average. In Figure 7.4, the long-term trend is represented by the 35-day moving average and the short-term trend is represented by the ten-day moving average. The shorter moving average always fluctuates more markedly than the longer one. Similar trading signals are generated by the MACD.

- A buy signal is given when the short-term moving average moves up and crosses over the long-term moving average from below.
- A sell signal is given when the short-term moving average moves down and crosses over the long-term moving average from above.

Another technique is to make a moving average of the daily highs and another moving average of the daily lows. This results in a band running across the bar chart or the candlestick chart. When the daily closing price moves outside this band, it is an indication that a new price trend may be developing.

Oscillators

Charts and moving averages tell us about the trend. Oscillators are tools that measure *momentum* or the rate of change in price movement. Their purpose is to identify over-bought and over-sold conditions. These conditions occur when momentum slows down near a top or bottom and the trend is getting ready to reverse direction. Two examples of oscillators are the relative strength indicator and the stochastic indicator.

The *relative strength indicator* is a measure of the rate of change in price movement. The rate of change can be either accelerating or decelerating. If the relative strength index moves above 80 per cent, it is considered over-bought and a top is forecast. If the relative strength index goes below 20 per cent, it is considered over-sold and a bottom is forecast.

The *stochastic indicator* is based on the premise that prices tend to accumulate near the upper end of their trading range in a rising market and near the lower end of their trading range in a falling market. When the stochastic indicator goes above 80 per cent, it is considered over-bought and a top is forecast. When the stochastic indicator goes below 20 per cent, it is considered over-sold and a bottom is forecast. However, in a strongly trending market, the stochastic indicator may remain in these extremes for some time.

Artificial intelligence

Identifying the exact means by which a technical trading system can be built and profitably exploited is like searching for the holy grail of investing. The reason that this type of analysis is so perplexing is because financial variables have a number of characteristics that make it difficult to pin them down. A new approach to evaluating these problems is to employ artificial intelligence techniques called *neural networks* and *genetic algorithms*. They are available as software packages that run on your personal computer. Some have interesting names such as NeuroForecaster, Stock Prophet, Brainmaker, NeuroWindows and Genetica. They have been used in a variety of applications, including stock price forecasting, stock selection, exchange rate forecasting, All Ordinaries Index forecasting, interest rate forecasting, bond rating analysis and futures trading.

Neural network

A neural network system allows the data itself to determine both the structure and the parameters of a trading system. It learns by example and adapts itself using a process of performance feedback. It is based on the same processes that go on in the human brain to solve complex tasks such as visual pattern recognition or learning a language. Creating a neural network consists of configuring the network and training it.

The result is a neural network that has learned the optimal combination of complex variables in predicting a specific outcome. It decides for itself which input variables are important and in what combination they are used to make a prediction. When it receives new data, it produces a judgement. It derives its forecasting powers by trial-and-error and it cannot actually tell us how the forecasts work. Some neural networks perform better than others, and the art of building good ones appears to be the way in which they are configured and trained.

Genetic algorithm

Genetic algorithms differ from neural networks because they deliver information not only about how to trade, but also why. Genetic algorithms are based on a computer simulation of Darwinian evolution theory. The parallel in financial forecasting is that every trading rule has a certain fitness in terms of its ability to contribute to a correct prediction. Over successive generations the stronger trading rules will survive and the weaker ones will not.

The genetic algorithm consists of a computer program that creates an environment in which trading rules compete and only the fittest survive. It generates and evaluates every possible trading rule associated with a particular data set and then combines the best ones together. By repeating this process many times, it evolves a trading system consisting of the strongest predictive variables in the correct combination.

By generating and testing a wide variety of trading scenarios, the genetic algorithm avoids the inflexibility traditionally associated with technical trading systems. Each trading scenario is able to compete with every other trading scenario and it is not easily distracted by the occasional disruptive influences that occur in financial markets. The forecasting effectiveness of genetic algorithms is only beginning to be explored. Its searching skills may help to unearth neglected or previously undiscovered technical trading systems.

Australian software suppliers

Technical analysis can be a labour-intensive activity because there are hundreds of stocks that you can follow and scores of complex technical trading systems. With improvements in computer technology, the availability of on-line data and the development of sophisticated software, private investors now have the same capability to engage in technical analysis as professional traders.

There are three types of computer packages. The first is designed to produce charts quickly and easily so that the user may make their own interpretation. The second goes a step further by calculating a number of technical indicators. The third goes even further by invoking a set of specified trading rules that automatically produce buy and sell signals. There are also software packages known as *black box* systems that produce buy and sell signals but don't tell you why. Pure charting packages are the least expensive. Packages that include technical indicators and trading systems become more expensive when they include more features. Most trading software is written for IBM-compatible personal computers running the *Windows* operating system. The following list consists of Australian software suppliers, their Internet addresses and the names of the software products they offer:

- ADEST http://www.adest.com.au: Cycletrader Wavetrader, Elwave, Ganntrader
- Archer Analysis http://www.archeranalysis.com: Bull's Eye Broker
- Beesoft http://www.beesoft.net: Pro TA
- Blaze Technology http://www.blazetech.com.au: Blaze Chart
- Bloomberg http://www.bloomberg.com.au: Bloomberg Professional
- Bourse Data http://www.bourseinvestor.com: Futures Trader, Personal Investor
- Bridge DFS http://www.dfs.com.au: IRESS, WebIRESS
- Brightspark http://www.bspark.com.au: Technifilter Plus
- Cycletrader Software http://www.cycletrader.com.au: Cycletrader Wavetrader
- Dial and Chart http://www.dialchart.com.au: Insight Trader
- Fibonacci Trader http://www.fibonaccitrader.com: Fibonacci Trader
- Harts Australasia http://www.hartsgroup.com: Harts Stockwatch
- Insight Trading http://www.insighttrading.com.au: Insight Trader
- Lincoln Indicators http://www.lincolnind.com.au: Stock-Doctor
- Market Analyst Software http://www.marketanalyst.com.au: Market Analyst II
- MarketCast http://www.marketcast.com.au: MarketCast Classic Suite, Market Detective

- MAUS Business Systems http://www.maus.com: Stockmarket Plus, OmniTrader
- Meta Share http://www.metashare.com: Metashare Advantage
- Micro Corporation http://www.microcorp.com.au: Blue Chip Trader
- Modernage http://www.tcompton.com: Trade Manager
- Netquote http://www.netquote.com.au: ASX Trademaster, StockEasy
- OTS Data http://www.ezycast.com: EzyStation, EsyChart, MetaStock
- Paritech http://www.paritech.com.au: Advanced GET, HotTrader, MetaStock, MetaMarket+, OmniTrader, StockDoctor
- Prognosis http://www.elwave.com: Elwave
- Proview http://www.proview.com.au: Proview Navigator
- QBL http://www.qbl.com.au: OptionStation, RadarScreen, TradeStation
- Quicken http://www.quicken.com.au: ShareAnalyser
- Share Graphics http://wwwsharegraphics.com: Pro Max 4, Pro Max 4 Plus
- Sharefinder http://www.sharefinder.com.au: Market Master, Market Partner, Sustained Profit Advantage
- STAG http://www.stagptyltd.com.au: STAG
- STEX Investor Software http://www.stex.com.au: Stex Charting
- Stockmarketearth.com http://www.stockmarketearth.com: Chart4Free, Chart4Free enhanced
- SuperTech Software http://www.supertech.com.au: StockMaster
- Trade Tech Online Australia http://www.tradetech.com.au: Market Analyser
- Weblink http://www.weblink.com.au: A&A Weblink

A good knowledge of technical analysis is important if you want to get the best results from these packages. Buying the software is only the first step; you also need to make an effort to fully understand how to use these programs to get your money's worth.

Australian data suppliers

Some software suppliers also sell data on-line, which virtually eliminates any compatibility problems and makes support easier. However, if you don't buy your data from your software supplier, then you need to be sure that the data is compatible with your software. Decide if you want cheaper end-of-day data or more expensive continuous data in real time. The following list consists of Australian data suppliers, their Internet addresses and the markets they cover:

- AAP Financial Markets http://www.aap.com.au: ASX, SFE, overseas
- ADEST http://www.adest.com.au: ASX, SFE, overseas
- Almax Information Systems http://www.almax.com.au: ASX, SFE, overseas
- Bourse Data http://www.bourseinvestor.com: ASX, SFE
- Bridge Information Systems http://www.bridge.com: ASX, SFE, overseas
- Charting Australia http://www.chartingaustralia.com.au: ASX, SFE
- DaytraderHQ http://www.daytraderhq.com: ASX, SFE, overseas
- Derivatives.com.au http://www.derivatives.com.au: ASX, SFE
- Dial & Chart http://www.dialchart.com.au: ASX, SFE, overseas
- FutureSource http://www.futuresource.com: SFE, overseas
- Hubb Organisation http://www.hubb.org: ASX, SFE, overseas
- Just Data http://www.justdata.com.au: ASX, SFE, overseas
- MarketCast http://www.marketcast.com.au: ASX, SFE
- MarketSource http://www.marketsource.net.au: ASX, SFE
- Netquote http://www.netquote.com.au: ASX
- OTS Data http://www.ezycast.com.au: ASX, SFE, overseas
- Paritech http://www.paritech.com.au: ASX, SFE, overseas
- Sharelink http://www.sharelink.com.au: ASX
- WebLink http://www.weblink.com.au: ASX, SFE

8

Debt securities

FEATURES OF DEBT SECURITIES 118
RATE OF RETURN IN DEBT SECURITIES 121
RISK IN DEBT SECURITIES 123
INTEREST RATES AND PRICE VOLATILITY 127
PASSIVE INVESTMENT STRATEGIES 130
ACTIVE INVESTMENT STRATEGIES 131

Debt securities differ from equity securities in a number of ways. Investors in debt securities are lenders or creditors, whereas equity investors are part owners. A debt security has a limited life or maturity, whereas an equity security has a continuous life. Investors in debt securities receive interest payments in which the amount and timing are known in advance, whereas equity investors generally receive dividends when and if they are declared.

Debt securities are issued by the Commonwealth government, state governments, semi-government agencies and companies. There are different types of debt securities that vary in terms of the issuer, risk, return, marketability, maturity and the frequency of interest payments. The purpose of this chapter is to describe the characteristics of debt securities, explain the nature of risk and return in debt securities, consider the effect of changes in interest rates on the prices of debt securities, and illustrate passive and active investment strategies in debt securities.

Features of debt securities

Access to the market for debt securities by small individual investors is limited. One reason is that small investors don't normally deal in the minimum amounts traded by financial institutions. Another reason is that many investors buy debt securities with a view to holding them until maturity, which substantially reduces the volume of trading in the secondary market. As a result, some investors prefer the interest-bearing alternatives to debt securities offered by banks, building societies and credit unions, such as savings accounts, interest-bearing cheque accounts, call deposits, fixed term deposits and cash management accounts.

Yields for government securities and bank accepted bills are generally published in the daily financial pages. Banks and other financial institutions can tell you about the rates they offer for various forms of deposits and the rates they can get for you on bank accepted bills. Your stockbroker will be able to advise you about the prices and yields for other listed and unlisted debt securities. You can buy some debt securities directly from the issuers such as finance companies, and Commonwealth government bonds can be bought from the Reserve Bank of Australia. There are a handful of stockbrokers who handle retail transactions in debt securities for individual investors.

There are several ways to describe the characteristics of negotiable debt securities. We shall divide debt securities into discount securities and fixed interest securities. Some of the basic elements that apply to all debt securities include:

- The amount of the loan is called its par value or *face value.*
- The interest rate is known as the *coupon rate.*
- The *interest dates* are when interest payments are made.
- The *maturity date* is when the issuer promises to repay the face value.
- The *market price* is determined by buyers and sellers and may be more or less than face value.
- The *yield* is the rate of return on a debt security.

Discount securities

Discount securities, as the name implies, are sold at a discount from their face value. They are traded in the *short-term money market*. The difference between the discount price and the face value represents the interest component which is realised when the security is resold or matures. Most discount securities have a maturity of six months or less. Discount securities include treasury notes, bank accepted bills of exchange, and zero-coupon or deep discount bonds. Cash management trusts are an alternative way for individuals to invest in discount securities.

Treasury notes are negotiable Commonwealth government securities that are issued weekly by tender through the Reserve Bank. They are issued for periods of five, thirteen or 26 weeks at a discount from face value. Competitive bidders in the primary market are mostly financial institutions; however, private investors are able to participate for a part of each issue in multiples of $5000 face value at the weighted average yield. Treasury notes can also be bought and sold at any time in the secondary market.

Bank accepted bills of exchange are negotiable short-term debt securities that are effectively guaranteed by a bank that has *accepted* them. Also included in this category are bank negotiable certificates of deposit. Bank bills and certificates of deposit are usually issued for maturities of five, 30, 60, 90 or 180 days at a discount from face value. They are traded in large amounts in the institutional money market, but smaller amounts can be bought and sold for individual investors through banks and stockbrokers. They are an alternative to fixed term deposits for investors who are looking for low risk.

Deep discount bonds are longer-term discount debt securities that either pay no interest at all or only a small nominal interest payment. A zero-coupon bond is the ultimate deep discount bond.

Cash management trusts and bank *cash management accounts* have become a popular way for small investors to gain access to the short-term money market. You can buy units in a cash management trust which in turn invests the money in Commonwealth treasury notes, bank bills and other highly liquid short-term debt securities. Alternatively, you can deposit funds into a bank cash management account that earns interest from investments in the short-term money market. You can invest modest sums of money and you can withdraw your funds at short notice. Some cash management facilities also offer cheque access. This is an attractive alternative to holding short-term funds in a deposit account that pays a low rate of interest.

Fixed interest securities

Fixed interest securities make interest payments at a fixed rate on specified dates. The face value is repayable at maturity. Fixed interest securities usually have longer maturities. The fixed interest securities that are of most interest to individual investors are Commonwealth treasury bonds, semi-government loans, mortgage-backed bonds, corporate debentures, unsecured notes, convertible notes, indexed bonds and floating rate notes.

Treasury bonds are Commonwealth government securities that are issued in multiples of $100 000 face value by tender through the Reserve Bank. However, private investors may buy and sell treasury bonds in multiples of $1000 face value through the Reserve Bank or a stockbroker. They pay interest half-yearly.

Semi-government bonds or notes are issued by state government central borrowing authorities and other authorities such as water boards, the Australian Wheat Board or the National Railways. They generally pay interest half-yearly and offer yields that are somewhat higher than equivalent Commonwealth government issues.

Mortgage-backed bonds are issued to finance, and are secured by, one or more first mortgages on property.

Debentures are corporate borrowings that are secured either by a fixed charge over specific assets of the company or by a floating charge over the unpledged assets of the company. They are generally issued in units of $100 face value and pay interest half-yearly, except for finance company debentures which pay interest quarterly. The yields on debentures are higher than for Commonwealth and semi-government securities because they represent greater risk. A trust deed provides for the appointment of a trustee to protect the debenture-holders' interests. Some debenture issues are listed on the ASX, but most are traded in the unlisted market.

Unsecured notes are also corporate borrowings that are generally issued in units of $100 face value. They tend to have a shorter maturity than debentures. Unsecured notes are also covered by a trust deed that is administered by an independent trustee, but they are not secured by a charge over any of the company's assets. If the company is ever wound up, unsecured note-holders rank behind the debenture-holders and consequently offer a higher yield as compensation. Some unsecured notes are listed on the ASX but most are traded in the unlisted market.

Convertible notes are corporate unsecured notes that are convertible into the company's ordinary shares at the discretion of the holder. They combine the advantages of a fixed interest security with the benefits of the ordinary share into which they may be converted. They offer a fixed interest return together with the potential for a capital gain if the underlying shares increase in price. Convertible notes may be listed on the ASX together with the underlying listed shares. *Converting notes* are similar to convertible notes except that they automatically convert into the company's shares under specified conditions.

Indexed bonds are debt securities that offer some degree of inflation protection. *Capital*-indexed bonds offer an adjustment in the face value based on changes in the Consumer Price Index. The fixed coupon rate is applied to the adjusted face value in calculating the interest payable. *Interest*-indexed bonds have a constant face value and the interest rate consists of a fixed component plus an indexed component equivalent to the Consumer Price Index rate of inflation. Investors who are concerned with maintaining a real rate of return over the inflation rate are sometimes attracted to indexed bonds.

Floating rate notes are debt securities that carry a variable interest rate that is adjusted regularly by a margin against a benchmark rate such as 90-day bank bills.

Rate of return in debt securities

An investor in a debt security knows in advance the face value and the coupon rate. Interest may be paid half-yearly or quarterly. The face value and the coupon rate are contractual obligations of the issuer that don't change. The market price of a debt security, however, will vary inversely with changes in the market rate of interest. Variations in the price of a debt security affect its expected rate of return or its *yield*. The concept of yield is critical to understanding debt securities and we shall focus on the *yield to maturity* and the *discount yield*.

Yield to maturity (YTM)

The yield to maturity, sometimes called the *promised yield*, is important for comparing the yields of debt securities with different prices, different coupon rates and different terms to maturity. It assumes that the security will be held to maturity and that the interest payments will be reinvested. The exact calculation requires a financial calculator or a computer. You can solve yield to maturity calculations by hand, however, by using the *approximate yield to maturity* formula.

$$\text{Approximate YTM} = \frac{\text{Annual interest payment} + \dfrac{\text{Face value} - \text{Current price}}{\text{Years to maturity}}}{\dfrac{\text{Face value} + \text{Current price}}{2}}$$

If a debenture with a face value of \$100, a coupon rate of 10 per cent and ten years term to maturity is selling for \$80, then the approximate yield to maturity is 13.33 per cent. It is greater than the coupon rate because it incorporates the effect of the \$20 discount in market price under face value.

$$\text{Approximate YTM} = \frac{\$10 + \dfrac{\$100 - \$80}{10}}{\dfrac{\$100 + \$80}{2}} = 13.33\%$$

If the market price for the debenture is \$120, then the yield to maturity is 7.27 per cent. In this case, the yield to maturity is lower than the coupon rate because it incorporates the effect of the \$20 premium in market price over face value.

$$\text{Approximate YTM} = \frac{\$10 + \frac{\$100 - \$120}{10}}{\frac{\$100 + \$120}{2}} = 7.27\%$$

Discount yield

Discount securities don't make periodic interest payments but are sold at a discount from face value. They are generally quoted in terms of their discount yield.

$$\text{Discount yield} = \frac{365 \text{ days}}{\text{Days to maturity}} \times \frac{\text{Face value} - \text{Market price}}{\text{Market price}}$$

A \$100 000 face value Commonwealth treasury note matures in 73 days and is currently selling for \$98 814. The discount yield is 6 per cent per annum.

$$\text{Discount yield} = \frac{365 \text{ days}}{73 \text{ days}} \times \frac{\$100\,000 - \$98\,814}{\$98\,814} = 6\%$$

Risk in debt securities

Compared with equity securities, debt securities generally carry a lower risk. Nevertheless, every debt security carries some degree of risk, including interest rate risk, reinvestment risk, inflation and taxes, credit risk, market liquidity and call risk.

Interest rate risk

The price of a debt security varies inversely with changes in the market rate of interest. Therefore, rising market interest rates result in lower prices for debt securities, and falling market interest rates result in higher prices for debt securities. You can suffer a capital loss if market rates of interest go up and you need to sell your debt securities before they mature. If market rates of interest go down, however, your debt securities will increase in price resulting in a capital gain. Interest rate risk is reflected in price volatility.

Reinvestment risk

When interest payments are received, they are normally reinvested unless the funds are required for some other purpose. If the market rate of interest goes down, then the interest payments will be reinvested at a lower rate. If the market rate of interest goes up, then the interest payments will be reinvested at a higher rate.

Inflation and taxes

The yield is your expected rate of return from an investment in a debt security. Inflation and taxes, however, erode your yield. If a debt security earns a 10 per cent yield and your marginal tax rate is 47 per cent, then your after-tax return is only 5.3 per cent. If inflation is more than 5.3 per cent, then your real return after tax is negative. That is why the prices of long-term debt securities decline rapidly when inflation rises, in order to make the yield more attractive.

The goal is to keep pace with inflation on an after-tax basis. You can calculate the breakeven interest rate by dividing the expected inflation rate by 100 per cent minus your tax rate. For example, if you are on the 47 per cent tax rate and you expect the inflation rate to average about 6 per cent, then your breakeven yield is 11.32 per cent.

$$\text{Breakeven yield} = \frac{\text{Expected inflation rate}}{100\% - \text{Tax rate}}$$

$$\frac{6\%}{100\% - 47\%} = 11.32\%$$

The higher the breakeven yield, the more risk you will bear. In extreme circumstances, you will need to choose between seeking the high-risk breakeven yield or simply minimising the loss to your spending power. Minimising the loss to your spending power can sometimes be a better alternative than risking the loss of your principal. Debt securities are not usually a good hedge against inflation. If you are worried about inflation, you may want to consider indexed bonds in which the principal or the interest payments are adjusted according to movements in the Consumer Price Index.

Credit risk

Credit risk refers to the ability of the issuer to make the interest payments and to repay the face value at maturity. Commonwealth securities carry virtually no risk of default. Semi-government securities carry a slight credit risk because they depend on the creditworthiness of the issuer. Corporate credit risks vary enormously and are affected by financial structure, profitability, cash flow management and the reliability of accounting practices.

Standard & Poor's and Moody's are two credit rating agencies that assess the credit risk of debt securities. They make an objective evaluation of a debt security and assign a letter rating to reflect their assessment. Credit rating agencies are independent of government, financial institutions and the borrowers. A credit rating reflects credit risk only and does not constitute a recommendation to buy or sell a particular security.

Figure 8.1 is an example of Standard & Poor's credit rating symbols. Long-term debt ratings are divided into two groups called *investment grade* and *speculative grade*. These are divided into a number of specific rating categories. Ratings from AA to CCC may be modified by the addition of a plus or minus sign to show relative standing within an individual category. Standard & Poor's also operates *CreditWatch* in which an issuer appears when an event has occurred, or is expected to occur, that may result in a positive or negative change to their credit rating.

If an issuer's credit risk increases, then their credit rating may be downgraded. Investors will react to a lower credit rating by demanding a greater yield to compensate for the increased risk. A greater yield can only be achieved by driving down the price. Credit ratings also help investors to evaluate the yield that they should expect before investing in a particular debt security.

Market liquidity

Market liquidity risk means that a debt security may be difficult to resell once you own it. This can be the result of too few buyers and sellers of that particular issue so that trading is infrequent or

Figure 8.1 Standard & Poor's credit ratings

Investment grade ratings

AAA	**Extremely strong** capacity to meet financial commitments. Highest rating.
AA	**Very strong** capacity to meet financial commitments.
A	**Strong** capacity to meet financial commitments, but somewhat more susceptible to adverse economic conditions and changes in circumstances.
BBB	**Adequate** capacity to meet financial commitments, but more subject to adverse economic conditions. Lowest investment grade rating.

Speculative grade gatings

BB	**Less vulnerable** in the near term but faces major ongoing uncertainties and exposures to adverse business, financial and economic conditions.
B	**More vulnerable** to adverse business, financial and economic conditions, but currently has the capacity to meet financial commitments.
CCC	**Currently vulnerable** and dependent on favourable business, financial and economic conditions to meet financial commitments.
CC	**Currently highly vulnerable.**
C	**A bankruptcy petition** has been filed or similar action taken, but payments or financial commitments are continued.
D	**Payment default** on financial commitments.

sporadic. In order to flush out a buyer, a seller may need to drop their price substantially. Similarly, dealers will quote a large spread between the bid price and the offer price in order to compensate themselves for making a market in such a thinly traded security. Moreover, it may take some time before a sale can be achieved. The more uncertainty about the time element and the price concession, the greater is market liquidity risk. The greater the market liquidity risk, the greater the required yield and the lower the market price.

Call risk

Call risk only applies to debt securities with a call provision. A call provision means that the issuer can repurchase the securities from investors before the maturity date at a specified price. For example, if market interest rates go below the coupon rate on a debenture issue, then the company may decide to call the debentures and issue new ones with a lower coupon rate. It is traditional for the call price to consist of face value plus a premium equivalent to one year's interest.

Call risk means that you may be forced to liquidate a high-yielding investment. Call risk is greatest when interest rates are high and expected to fall. Under these circumstances, you would either avoid debt securities with a call provision or you would expect an increased *yield to call* to compensate you for call risk. When interest rates are expected to rise, yield differentials for call risk are negligible.

Interest rates and price volatility

The main reason that the prices of debt securities fluctuate is due to changes in the market rate of interest. Inasmuch as the Commonwealth government has considerable influence over interest rates through monetary and fiscal policies, any expected changes in those policies will affect the market prices for debt securities.

Despite attempts to forecast the direction and magnitude of movements in interest rates, many of the economic and political variables that affect interest rates are essentially unpredictable. What is more useful for the individual investor is the ability to interpret events as they unfold. Getting a grip on the nature of interest rates means understanding the significance of the yield curve, how changes to interest rates occur, and how interest rate changes affect the prices of debt securities.

Yield curve

A yield curve relates the yields for debt securities that are comparable in all respects except their term to maturity. The yield curve is a snapshot of the *term structure* of interest rates at a point in time, and it can be used to anticipate the effects of changes in interest rates on the prices of debt securities.

The normal or *ascending* yield curve consists of rising yields as maturities become longer. It is the most common shape of the yield curve and it tends to prevail when market interest rates are moderate or low. Generally, the longer the maturity, the higher the yield, because there is more uncertainty about potential long-term changes to interest rates, inflation and the credit risk of the issuers. Figure 8.2 on page 133 is an example of an ascending yield curve.

The *descending* yield curve consists of falling yields as maturities become longer. It is not very common and tends to occur when short-term market interest rates are relatively high. The descending yield curve is strong evidence of intervention by the Reserve Bank. The slope of the yield curve usually flattens out for longer maturities so that yield differentials become insignificant.

When the term structure of interest rates changes, the yield curve is not only capable of shifting up and down, but it can also change shape. Short-term interest rates are essentially the Reserve Bank's monetary policy instrument for controlling liquidity in the economy. The cost of short-term funds forms the foundation of the interest rate structure that flows through to the cost of longer-term debt securities. A neutral or loose monetary policy results in an ascending yield curve, and a tight monetary policy results in a descending yield curve.

Interest rate movements

In determining a short-term interest rate target, the Reserve Bank examines the performance of a list of economic and financial variables. The relative weighting given to each variable depends on how important it is regarded at different phases of the business cycle.

- inflation
- growth of the money supply
- exchange rate of the Australian dollar
- current account deficit
- retail sales

- expected investment
- labour market trends
- housing starts and new finance
- consumer confidence
- business confidence

Short-term interest rates are essentially controlled by the Reserve Bank, but longer-term interest rates tend to float more freely according to the supply and demand for long-term funds and the expectations for inflation. Long-term funds are needed by the Commonwealth, state and local governments, and the corporate sector. The sources of long-term funds are the domestic household sector and overseas lenders. Therefore, anything that affects the supply and demand for long-term funds will affect long-term interest rates, such as changes in household savings, the level of investment, taxation incentives, expected inflation and Reserve Bank monetary policy. Expectations are probably more important than actual changes in explaining the day-to-day volatility of long-term interest rates.

Overseas interest rates also affect the level of interest rates in Australia. The Reserve Bank can only set domestic interest rates as long as the Australian dollar is allowed to float freely. When the Reserve Bank tries to hold the exchange rate at any particular level, by intervening in the foreign exchange market, it is forced to maintain a differential with overseas interest rates. The result is a loss of control over domestic interest rates. Therefore, the level of overseas interest rates plays a big part in determining interest rates in Australia.

Price volatility

The prices of debt securities vary inversely with changes in market rates of interest. If market interest rates rise and the yield curve shifts upwards, then the prices of debt securities will fall. If market interest rates fall and the yield curve shifts downwards, then the prices of debt securities will rise. However, the degree of price volatility is also affected by the term to maturity, the coupon rate and the overall level of market interest rates.

All other things equal, a change in the market rate of interest will result in greater price volatility to the extent that a debt security's maturity is longer, the coupon rate is lower, and the market rate of interest from which a change begins is higher. Conversely, a change in the market rate of interest will result in less price volatility to the extent that a debt security's maturity is shorter, the coupon rate is higher, and the market rate of interest from which a change begins is lower. The practical implications of these principles are important when it comes to making investment decisions in debt securities.

- In order to maximise capital gains from falling market interest rates, choose high price-volatility debt securities that have long maturities and low coupon rates.
- In order to minimise capital losses from rising market interest rates, choose low price-volatility debt securities that have short maturities and high coupon rates.
- Keep in mind that price volatility in debt securities is greater when market interest rates are high and less when market interest rates are low.

Passive investment strategies

Passive debt investment strategies are characterised by the fact that they make no judgements about future interest rates. Passive investors are generally long-term investors who are not actively seeking to improve their returns beyond the market yield. Passive investment strategies are still concerned with identifying and monitoring the risk and return tradeoffs that match an investor's objectives. Passive investment strategies consist of buy-and-hold and laddering.

A buy-and-hold strategy simply consists of buying securities that meet your investment criteria and holding them until they mature. Short-term cash flow requirements can be invested in short-term securities, and long-term cash flow requirements can be matched with longer-term maturities. A buy-and-hold strategy minimises interest rate risk, but it does not protect you from other forms of risk.

If you choose maturities that are very long, you will generally get higher yields. But you also run the risk of loss of principal if market interest rates rise, prices decline and you need to sell before maturity. If you choose maturities that are very short, you will preserve your principal but you will generally get lower yields.

Another strategy for protecting against interest rate risk is to *ladder* your maturities. This consists of placing equal investments into evenly spaced maturities. Not only will the returns be an average between the short-term and long-term yields, but also an average of market yields over time. Proceeds from interest payments and maturing securities are reinvested in longer-dated securities in order to maintain the laddering of maturities. Laddering also offers greater liquidity than a buy-and-hold strategy because a portion of the portfolio is always maturing.

An alternative form of the laddering strategy is to use only one short-term maturity and one long-term maturity. By eliminating intermediate-term maturities, you obtain increased liquidity from the short-dated securities and increased returns from the long-dated securities.

Active investment strategies

Active debt investment strategies are characterised by the fact that they do make forecasts about future interest rates and use these forecasts in an attempt to produce additional returns. Active strategies are also higher-risk strategies because interest rate forecasting is a notoriously difficult task. These are generally short-term strategies that require continual monitoring and more frequent trading. Active investment strategies consist of riding the yield curve and interest rate swaps.

The yield curve depicts changes in the yield to maturity from short-term securities to long-term securities that are identical in all other respects. A normal yield curve slopes upward as the term to maturity increases, reflecting higher yields on longer-term securities. As long as the yield curve remains normal, we can increase the returns on short-term investments by engaging in a strategy called *riding the yield curve*.

This is a strategy for investors who are primarily interested in minimum risk and maximum liquidity. It enables them to gain an improvement in the yield by buying debt securities further out on the yield curve, riding them down the slope, and then rolling them over again. Figure 8.2 and the following example illustrate the principle of riding the yield curve.

An investor is considering the purchase of a $100 000 face value, 90-day bank bill that is selling for $98 303. The discount yield on this bank bill is 7 per cent.

$$\text{Discount yield} = \frac{365 \text{ days}}{90 \text{ days}} \times \frac{\$100\ 000 - \$98\ 303}{\$98\ 303} = 7\%$$

At the same time, a 180-day bank bill is selling for $96 205 with a discount yield of 8 per cent.

$$\text{Discount yield} = \frac{365 \text{ days}}{180 \text{ days}} \times \frac{\$100\ 000 - \$96\ 205}{\$96\ 205} = 8\%$$

Figure 8.2 Riding the yield curve

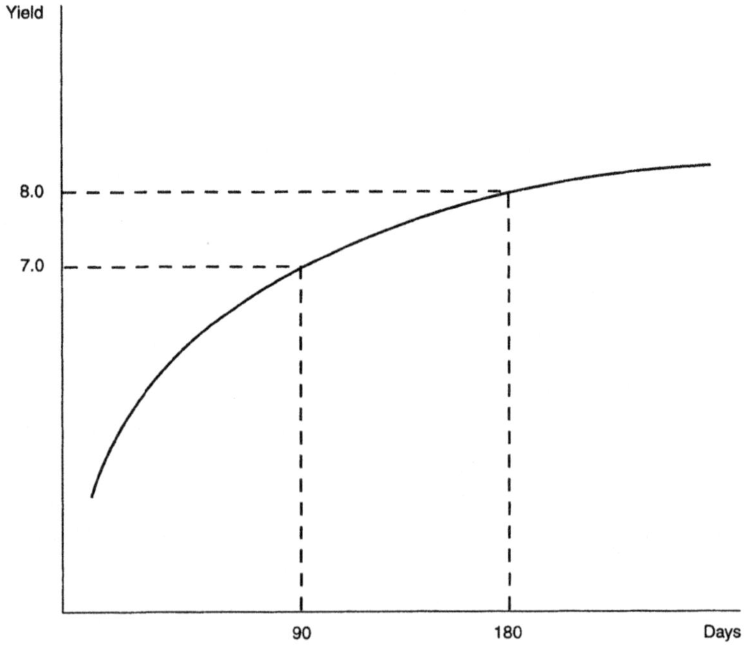

If the investor believes that the yield curve won't change, then buying the 180-day bank bill and reselling it at the end of 90 days will result in a better return.

$$\text{Discount yield} = \frac{365 \text{ days}}{90 \text{ days}} \times \frac{\$98\ 303 - \$96\ 205}{\$96\ 205} = 8.84\%$$

Riding the yield curve in this way produces an 8.84 per cent discount yield. What happens, however, if the yield curve does not remain stable? In the worst case, the investor can hold the 180-day bank bill to maturity, realising an 8 per cent discount yield. Riding the yield curve with minimum risk means that you need to be able to hold on until maturity if it becomes necessary.

Interest rate swaps represent a more aggressive strategy for investing in debt securities. They consist of selling one debt security and buying another to take advantage of mispricing or expected changes in the term structure of interest rates. There are four main types of interest rate swaps:

- The *yield swap* consists of selling a lower-yielding security and buying a higher-yielding security of the same quality and maturity. The motive is to exploit the mispricing of one or the other security in order to obtain a better yield.
- The *substitution swap* is a different approach to exploiting mispricing. It involves buying the higher-yielding security in the expectation that its yield is too high and will fall to that of the other security. The objective is to benefit from the increase in price that will accompany a fall in the yield.
- The *intersector swap* is based on mispricing between different sectors of the debt securities market. For example, if you think that the spread between yields on Commonwealth bonds and semi-government bonds is too wide and will narrow, you would swap from the lower-yielding Commonwealth bonds to the higher-yielding semi-government bonds.
- The *rate anticipation swap* is based on forecasting changes in market interest rates. If market interest rates are expected to rise, long-dated securities are swapped into short-dated securities in order to minimise the effects of a decline in price. If market interest rates are expected to decline, short-dated securities are swapped into long-dated securities to maximise the effect of an increase in price.

9

Derivatives

EQUITY OPTIONS	135
BUYING A CALL	141
BUYING A PUT	142
SELLING A CALL	144
SELLING A PUT	145
WARRANTS	147
FUTURES CONTRACTS	150
FUTURES TRADING	154

A *derivative* is a financial instrument that represents a claim on another asset. The value of a derivative is directly linked to the value of the underlying asset. The big difference is that a derivative is highly leveraged. Derivatives appear in a variety of forms and are traded on the Australian Stock Exchange, the Sydney Futures Exchange and the over-the-counter market. A lot has been written about the abuses of derivative securities. However, they are a legitimate investment medium that may appeal to more aggressive investors and they can also be used to hedge against risk for more conservative investors. Derivatives are complex investments that need to be fully understood before taking the plunge. Most of the trading in the Australian Stock Exchange Derivatives (ASXD) market is conducted in put and call options on a selected number of listed shares. Futures contracts and futures options trade on the SFE.

Equity options

Equity option contracts on the shares of about 50 companies, in addition to index options on the ASX200 Index, trade on the ASXD. These option contracts are standardised, which means that they conform to a set of specifications that are prescribed by the Exchange. An equity option contract conveys to its buyer, or *holder*, the right, but not the obligation, to trade in the underlying shares at a specified price on or before the expiry date. This right is granted by the seller, or *writer*, of the option.

- A *call option* conveys the right to *purchase* 1000 underlying shares. If you exercise a call, the writer is obliged to sell them to you at the exercise price.
- A *put option* conveys the right to *sell* 1000 underlying shares. If you exercise a put, the writer is obliged to buy them from you at the exercise price.

Figure 9.1 represents a newspaper quotation for call options on ABC shares.

Expiry

The *expiry date* occurs on the Thursday before the last Friday of the contract month. The option-holder must decide by the expiry date whether to resell the option, exercise it or allow it to lapse. ASXD equity options are *American-style* options, which means that they can be exercised at any time up to and including the expiry date. A *European-style* option can only be exercised on the expiry date. Options begin trading about nine months before the expiry date, and three *contract months* usually trade simultaneously. In Figure 9.1, ABC call options are trading in three contract months—December, March and June. When the December contract expires, September contracts begin trading.

Strike price

The *strike price*, also called the *exercise price*, is the share price at which an option can be exercised. For each contract month,

Figure 9.1 Call option quotation

CALL OPTIONS

Expiry	Strike price	Buyer	Seller	Last sale	Volume (000's)	Open interest	Implied volatility Buyer	Implied volatility Seller	Delta	Annual % return
ABC last sale price $2.86										
Dec	2.75	.14	.15	.14	90	3849	20.0	25.5	+.79	23.20
Dec	3.00	.03	.05	.04	50	1089	25.8	33.5	+.29	23.20
Mar	2.75	.24	.28	.25	40	3088	21.0	27.7	+.70	15.95
Mar	3.00	.13	.16	.15	32	1490	24.4	29.0	+.47	15.95
Mar	3.50	.03	.05	.03	5	3310	25.7	32.0	+.16	4.25
Jun	3.00	.21	.25	.23	10	270	25.1	29.8	+.53	13.91
Jun	3.50	.08	.11	.09	20	–	26.8	31.0	+.27	6.04

strike prices are set at intervals above and below the current market price of the underlying share. As the share price moves, new strike prices become available so that more volatile shares will have options with a greater range of strike prices. There are matching puts and calls for every contract month and strike price.

If the current market price of the underlying share is *greater* than the strike price, then a call option is said to be *in-the-money* because the holder can buy the underlying share for less than its current market value. If the current market price of the underlying share is *less* than the strike price, then a call option is *out-of-the-money*. If the strike price is equal to the market price of the underlying shares, a call option is said to be *at-the-money*. In Figure 9.1, ABC December call options are trading with strike or strike prices at $2.75 and $3. The Dec 275 call is in-the-money and the ABC Dec 300 call is out-of-the-money. The opposite conditions apply to put options.

Premium

The price paid for an option is called the *premium*. It should not be confused with the strike price or the price of the underlying shares. Option premiums are quoted on a per share basis. In Figure 9.1, the *Buyer* is the highest premium currently bid to buy ABC calls, the *Seller* is the lowest premium at which ABC calls are currently offered for sale, and the *Last sale* is the premium at which the closing trade occurred. The ABC Jun 300 call is bid at 21 cents per share, offered at 25 cents per share, and the last sale was at 23 cents per share. The *volume* of trading in ABC Jun 300 calls is ten contracts, each representing 1000 ABC shares, and the *open interest* or number of calls outstanding is 270 contracts.

Implied volatility

The two columns for *Implied volatility* in Figure 9.1 are an output of the Black-Scholes Option Pricing Model in which the underlying share price, option premium, strike price, time to expiry and interest rate are used to find the standard deviation of the underlying share's returns. It is calculated for the buyer's bid price and the seller's offer price.

Delta

The column for *Delta* in Figure 9.1 is a measure of the sensitivity of the option premium to changes in the underlying share price. For example, if a call premium increases by 5 cents when the underlying share price increases by 10 cents, then the delta ratio is .50. It tells us how much an option's premium should rise or fall given a change in the underlying share price. It also provides a relative measure of risk for different options on the same share. You can see from Figure 9.1 that in-the-money options have higher deltas and out-of-the-money options have lower deltas. Delta is also affected by the amount of time to expiry. Call options have a positive delta and put options have a negative delta.

Annual % return

The column for *Annual % return* in Figure 9.1 is the annualised rate of return to a covered call writer from the premium received if the option is held to expiry and the share price remains the same.

Adjustments

The strike price and/or the number of underlying shares will be adjusted to reflect the effects of any bonus issues, cash issues, consolidations or capital reconstructions. The idea is that an option-holder should not be disadvantaged when changes occur to the capital structure of the company. No adjustment is made, however, as a result of the declaration of a dividend. Cash dividends paid on the underlying shares affect the option premium through the ex dividend effect on the share price. Since the share price is expected to fall by the amount of the cash dividend, a cash dividend implies a lower call premium and a higher put premium.

Closing out

There are a number of ways to terminate or *close out* an option. One way is to exercise an option. You can also close out by making an offsetting transaction or allow the option to expire.

- To *exercise* an option, the purchase or sale of the underlying shares takes place at the strike price and the share position is liquidated to realise the gain or loss.
- Option gains or losses may also be realised at any time before expiration by making a *closing transaction* consisting of reselling a bought option or buying back a sold option.
- If an option is out-of-the-money at expiration, it automatically expires worthless.
- If an option is in-the-money at expiration, it is automatically exercised.

Valuation

The option premium is the only part of an option contract that is not standardised. There are six elements that are responsible for determining the premium for an equity option. They can be divided into *intrinsic value* and *time value.*

Intrinsic value	1. Underlying share price
	2. Strike price
Time value	3. Time remaining until expiry
	4. Volatility of the underlying share
	5. Level of market interest rates
	6. Expected dividends

Only in-the-money options have intrinsic value. The greater the intrinsic value, the greater the option premium.

- A *call* option has intrinsic value when the price of the underlying share is *greater* than the strike price.
- A *put* option has intrinsic value when the price of the underlying share is *less* than the strike price.

All options have time value until they expire. For in-the-money options, time value is the difference between the option premium and its intrinsic value. Out-of-the-money options consist only of time value. Options are frequently described as a *wasting* asset because they lose time value as they approach expiry. As a rough guide, an option will lose about one-third of its time value during the first half of its life and two-thirds of its time value during the second half of its life.

- The more time remaining until expiry, the greater the time value and hence the higher the option premium. The reason is because there is more time for the underlying share price to move into a position that makes the option profitable.
- The more volatile the underlying share price, the greater the time value and hence the higher the option premium. The reason is because greater volatility increases the possibility that the underlying share price will fluctuate into a profitable position.
- Higher interest rates generally result in higher call option premiums and lower put option premiums. The reason is that the level of interest rates represents the carrying charge for controlling the underlying shares.
- When the underlying shares go ex dividend, the share price will fall by the amount of the dividend. A call option premium will fall and a put option premium will rise proportionally to the amount of the dividend.

The elements that drive the option premium can be tied together mathematically using the *Black-Scholes Option Pricing Model*. Its purpose is to establish a *fair value* for a call option premium. Different versions of the model are used for a variety of option contracts. It is a rather daunting equation that does not easily lend itself to manual calculation. Fortunately, there are computer packages that will do the calculations by simply entering the variables.

The most difficult variable to determine is volatility. We can measure the historical standard deviation of share returns; however, we cannot be certain that it will be the same in the future. Alternatively, we can measure the *implied volatility* that equates the theoretical option premium to the current market premium using the Black-Scholes Option Pricing Model.

Buying a call

Buying a call is a strategy designed to benefit from an increase in the price of the underlying share. Your potential loss is limited to the amount you pay for the call premium if the price of the underlying share does not increase. The potential reward, however, is virtually unlimited. Figure 9.2 is the profit profile for buying a call. The vertical axis represents the gain or loss on the call option premium, and the horizontal axis represents the corresponding price of the underlying share.

Figure 9.2 Buying a call

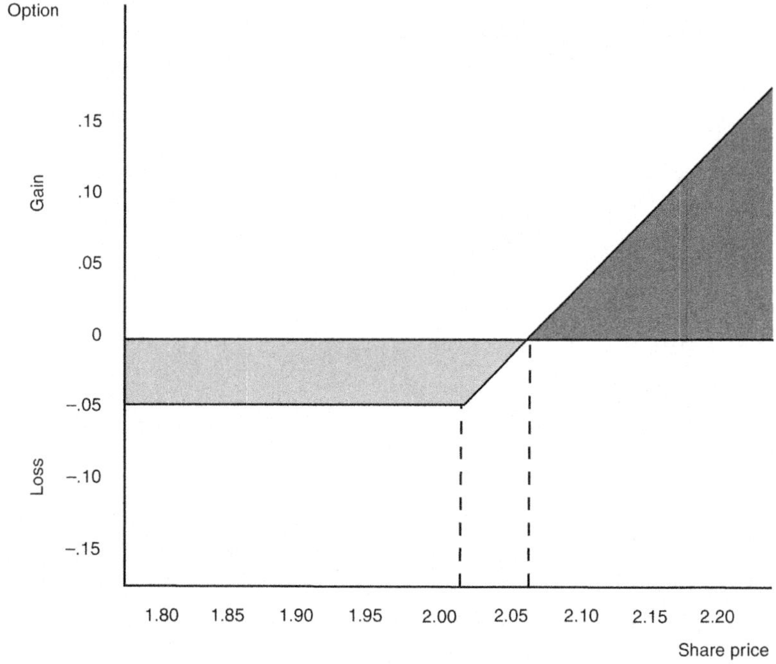

In this example, the call begins at-the-money in which both the current price of the underlying share and the strike price is \$2. The call option premium is 5 cents per share or \$50 for one contract.

- The amount of the call premium is your maximum potential loss if the price of the underlying share falls below the strike price.
- You will break even if the price of the underlying share rises above the strike price by the amount of the premium to \$2.05.
- Your potential profit is unlimited and depends on the extent to which the price of the underlying share rises above the breakeven point.

Leverage is one of the big attractions for buying options. Consider the difference between investing in shares at a market price of \$2, or buying a call on the same shares with a strike price of \$2 for a premium of 5 cents per share. If the share price increases by \$1 to \$3, the return on an investment in the shares is 50 per cent. At the same time, the call premium will also increase by \$1, resulting in an increase on the call premium of 2000 per cent.

Some investors buy calls as part of an overall investment plan. A popular strategy consists of placing 10 per cent of their funds into calls on selected shares and the other 90 per cent into low-risk debt securities. This strategy enables them to benefit from an increase in share prices while limiting downside risk to the call premium less the interest earned on the debt securities. Other investors use calls to lock in a purchase price until they have sufficient cash available to pay for the purchase.

Buying a put

Buying a put is a strategy designed to benefit from a fall in the price of the underlying share. Your risk is limited to the amount you pay for the put premium. The potential reward depends on how far the underlying share price falls. Put options provide a more attractive method than short selling because they offer not only greater leverage, but also a known and predetermined risk.

Figure 9.3 represents the profit profile for buying a put. In this example, the put begins at-the-money in which both the current price of the underlying share and the strike price is \$2. The put option premium is 5 cents per share or \$50 for one contract.

Figure 9.3 Buying a put

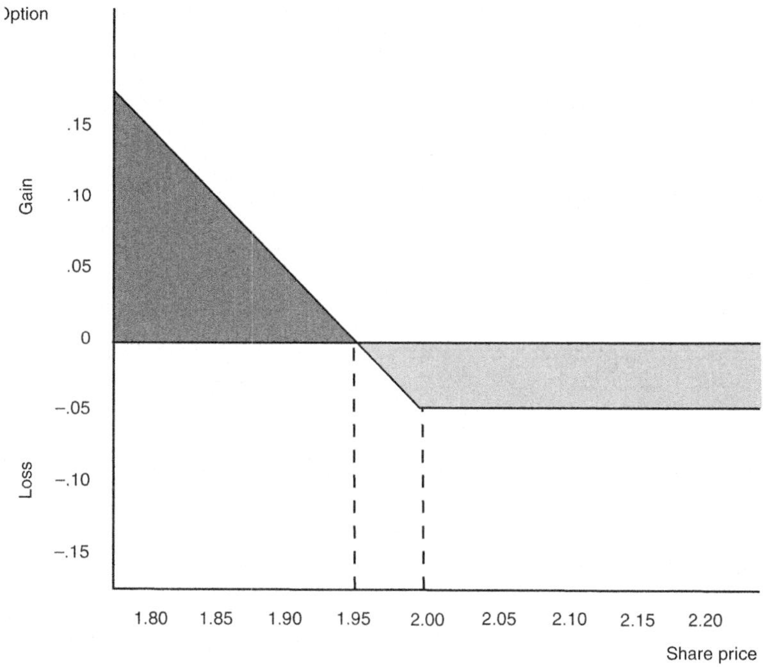

- The amount of the put premium is your maximum potential loss if the price of the underlying share remains greater than the strike price.
- You will break even if the price of the underlying shares falls below the strike price by the amount of the premium to \$1.95.
- Your potential profit depends on the extent to which the price of the underlying share falls below the breakeven point.

Some investors limit the risk of owning shares by simultaneously buying a put over them. This strategy limits their risk by establishing a minimum selling price for the shares and yields a profit to the extent that the share price increases by more than the put premium. The same strategy can be used to protect unrealised profits.

Selling a call

Selling a call, also known as *writing* a call, is a strategy designed to benefit from a fall in the price of the underlying share. A call seller is obligated to sell the underlying shares at the strike price if they are assigned an exercise notice to do so. For assuming this obligation, the call seller receives the call premium. A call seller holds the opposite view to a call buyer about the likely future price of the underlying shares.

Figure 9.4 is the profit profile for selling a call. In this example, the call begins at-the-money in which both the current price of the underlying share and the strike price is $2. The call option premium is 5 cents per share or $50 for one contract.

- The amount of the call premium is the maximum potential profit if the price of the underlying share remains below the strike price until expiry.
- The trade will break even if the price of the underlying shares rises above the strike price by the amount of the premium to $2.05.
- Potential losses are virtually unlimited and depend on the extent to which the price of the underlying share rises above the breakeven point.

The risks involved in selling a call depend on whether or not the call is *covered*. A covered call-writing strategy consists of selling a call on underlying shares that you already own. It enables you to earn income equal to the call premium, resulting in either additional returns or a cushion against a price decline in the underlying share. If the underlying share price increases substantially, however, the holder will call them away from you at the strike price. Covered call writing is a much more conservative strategy compared with uncovered call writing.

Selling at-the-money or in-the-money calls generates higher premium income, but it also gives up a larger proportion of the upside potential from holding the shares. Selling out-of-the-money calls generates less premium income, but it enables you to retain some participation in any rise in the share price.

The objective of selling an uncovered call is also to realise premium income but without owning the underlying shares.

Figure 9.4 Selling a call

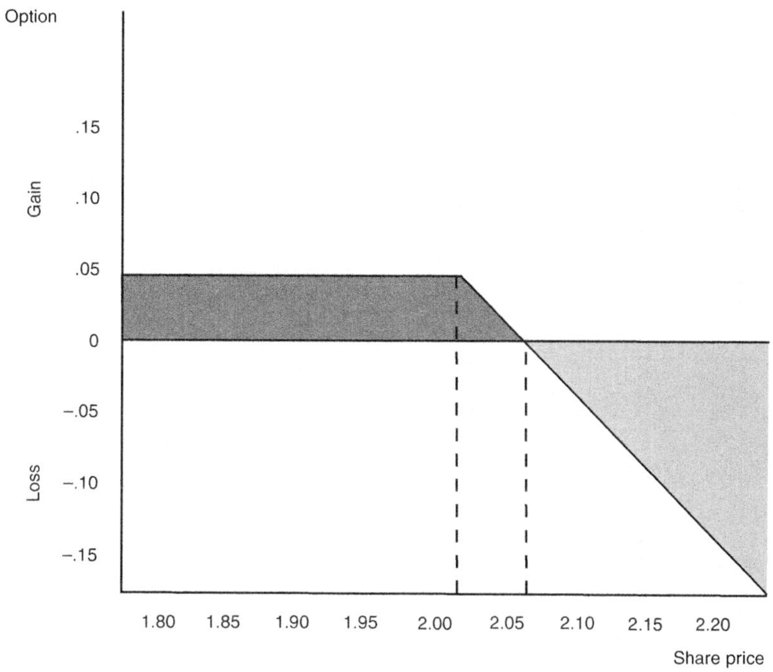

Uncovered options are also called *naked* options. An uncovered call writer must deposit and maintain sufficient margin with their stockbroker to ensure that they can acquire the underlying shares if the call is exercised. The risk is similar to short selling except that it is cushioned by the premium income.

Selling a put

Selling a put, also called *writing* a put, is perhaps the least understood of the four basic option strategies. Selling a put is a strategy designed to benefit from an increase in the price of the underlying share. As a put writer, you are obligated to buy the underlying shares at the strike price if you are assigned an exercise notice to do so. For assuming this obligation, you receive the put premium. A put seller holds the opposite view to the put

Figure 9.5 Selling a put

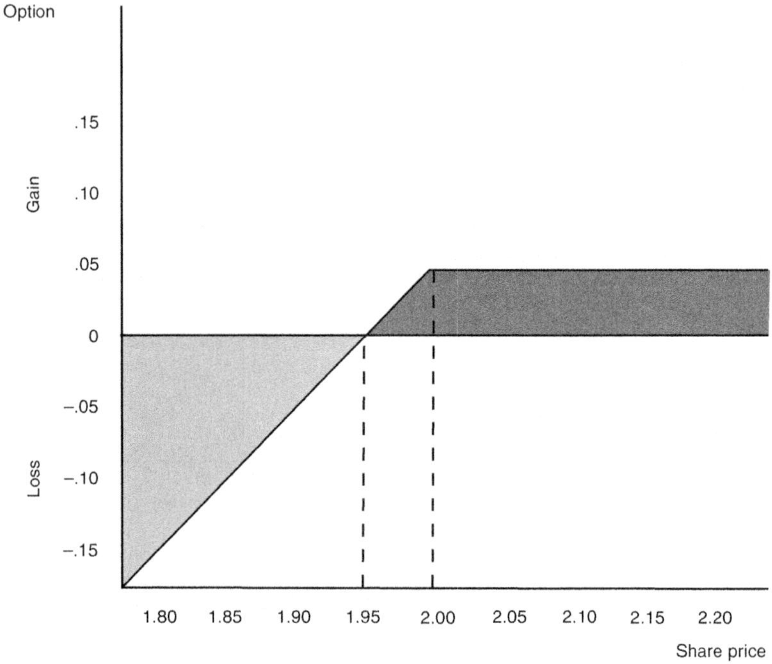

buyer about the likely future price of the underlying asset. Figure 9.5 is the profit profile for selling a put.

In this example, the put begins at-the-money in which both the current price of the underlying shares and the strike price is $2. The put option premium is 5 cents per share or $50 for one contract.

- The amount of the put premium is the maximum potential profit if the price of the underlying share remains above the strike price until expiry.
- You will break even if the price of the underlying share falls below the strike price by the amount of the premium to $1.95.
- Potential losses are virtually unlimited and depend on the extent to which the price of the underlying share falls below the breakeven point.

The risks involved in selling puts also depend on whether or not the put is covered. A covered put-writing strategy consists of having a corresponding short position in the underlying shares. An uncovered or naked put seller does not have a corresponding short position in the shares, so they must deposit sufficient margin with their stockbroker.

Warrants

A warrant is essentially a long-term option that is issued by a third party and traded on the ASX. Warrants are not a contract created by the ASX, nor are they guaranteed by the ASX. They are generally issued by large financial institutions, which means that the warrant-holder is exposed to the financial and business risks associated with the warrant-issuer. The issuer is the only party that can write a warrant.

Warrants are not standardised contracts, so the *terms of issue* may vary considerably from one warrant to another. They may be written over shares, a portfolio of shares, indexes, currencies, loan securities or commodities. They may be American-style or European-style, and delivery may be settled in cash or the underlying securities. Warrants don't have to be exercised to realise a profit as long as they can be resold; however, market liquidity for some warrants is not good.

The warrant premium is affected by a number of factors in common with other types of options. These include the current price and price volatility of the underlying asset, the level of interest rates, the strike price and the time to expiry. Since they are essentially long-term options, warrants are more expensive than standard equity options because of the time value component. Warrant premiums may also be affected by other factors, including the credit risk of the issuer, extraordinary events affecting the terms of issue, possible illiquidity in the secondary market, and potential adjustments resulting from a bonus share issue, a rights issue or a dividend payment. The *Offering Circular* and the *Terms of Issue* contain the specifications for each warrant and they may be structured in a variety of ways.

Call equity warrants and *put equity warrants* are issued over some of the shares listed on the ASX. They are the most common type of warrant traded. The strike price is usually close to the share price at the time of issue. They can be American-style or European-style, and the expiry date generally varies from six months to three years. If they are exercised, settlement may be in cash or delivery of the underlying shares. An issuer is not necessarily obliged to hold the underlying shares in order to issue the warrants. *Fully covered equity warrants*, however, are equity warrants in which the issuer has placed the underlying shares into a trust or similar arrangement in order to guarantee delivery if the warrant-holder chooses to exercise. The purpose of fully covered equity warrants is to reduce the issuer risk to the warrant-holder.

Some warrants are *capped*, in which the upside potential is limited. These warrants typically have a low strike price with European-style expiry. If the value of the underlying share is less than the cap level on expiry, the holder may exercise the warrant for its full value. If the value of the underlying share is greater than the cap level, however, then the holder may only receive the cap amount. For example, if the underlying shares are selling for $7 at expiry and the warrant is capped at $6 per share, then the issuer is only obliged to pay the holder the equivalent of $6 per share in cash or shares.

An *instalment warrant* is a call warrant that gives the holder the right to buy the underlying shares by making one or more subsequent payments during the life of the warrant. The buyer pays an initial instalment of about half of the current share price and becomes entitled to the capital gains and dividends in the underlying shares. If an instalment warrant is not exercised or the final payment is not made, then the shares are sold and the proceeds, less the final instalment, are paid to the holder. Instalment warrants are typically fully covered.

The *premium income equity* (PIE) warrant has some features in common with capped warrants, in addition to some of the features of instalment warrants. PIE warrants are typically issued over a parcel of shares with a value of $5000. Holders pay most of this price initially and have the right to purchase the parcel for a low strike price such as $1. The warrant-holder receives the dividends and franking credits on the shares together with a further distribution called *premium income*. The upside potential is capped at a designated price ceiling, making a PIE warrant similar to buying the shares and selling a call against them. For example, suppose you pay $5000 for a PIE warrant covering 1000 shares that are currently selling for $5. The terms of issue include a price ceiling of $7 and an entitlement to premium income of 6 per cent of $5000 together with the dividends and franking credits. If the shares are selling for $7 at expiry, then you will receive 1000 shares valued at $7000. If, however, the shares are selling for $10 at expiry, then you will receive only 700 shares valued at $7000.

An *endowment warrant* is a call warrant that gives the holder the opportunity to buy the underlying shares with their own dividends. These are usually European-style warrants with a ten-year expiry from the date of issue. Rather than a fixed strike price, they have an *outstanding amount* that is established when they are issued and which changes over time. The outstanding amount is reduced by the dividends paid on the underlying shares, and increased by an interest charge on the unpaid balance. Sometimes franking credits are also applied to the outstanding amount. The objective of an endowment warrant is to reduce the outstanding amount to zero by the expiry date and take delivery of the underlying shares. Whether this will actually happen depends on the amount of dividends received and the amount of interest charged. If an outstanding amount remains at expiry, then the holder must pay it off in order to take delivery of the underlying shares.

Low exercise price warrants are generally European-style warrants with a strike price of 1 cent. The buyer effectively pays the full value of the underlying shares. The difference between the warrant premium and the price of the underlying share is a function of the expected change in the share price by the time expiry occurs.

A *capital plus warrant* covers a portfolio of securities and is usually issued for $1000 each. These are European-style warrants with a term to expiry of about five years. The *capital plus* feature means that you are guaranteed to get your original $1000 back at expiry. In exchange for the capital guarantee, however, you are only entitled to a proportion, generally between 10 per cent and 30 per cent, of any increase in value. Some capital plus warrants are settled with the underlying shares and others are cash settled. The market price of the warrant will rise and fall with expectations about the underlying shares.

The value of an *index warrant* is linked to a price index such as the ASX200 Index. The strike price is expressed in points, and settlement is usually in cash. The amount of the settlement is calculated by multiplying the difference between the closing index and the strike price by a predetermined multiplier that converts the points into dollars. Some index warrants also have *barrier features* which, if triggered, cause the warrant to terminate early.

Put and call *currency warrants* entitle the holder to exchange an amount of foreign currency for Australian dollars. The warrants rise and fall according to movements in the Australian dollar against the foreign currency with reference to the strike price. For example, a holder of a $A/$US call warrant will benefit from a rise in the $A/$US exchange rate, and a holder of a put warrant will benefit from a fall in the exchange rate.

Futures contracts

A futures contract is a legally binding agreement to buy or sell a standard quantity of an underlying asset on a future date for a price agreed upon today. The underlying asset may be a physical commodity such as wool, wheat, oil, gold or electricity, or it may be a financial instrument such as a debt security, a stockmarket index or individual company shares. A futures contract is standardised in all respects except for the price, which is determined in the market between the buyer and the seller. The following terms are uniform in a futures contract.

Contract unit	The quantity of the underlying asset covered by one contract.
Delivery	The quality of the underlying asset which may be delivered. Sometimes delivery may be for an equivalent amount of cash.
Quotation	The way in which the contract price will be quoted, including the minimum fluctuation.
Contract months	The month in which a contract becomes deliverable. A futures contract may trade simultaneously in several contract months.
Termination	The day on which trading terminates.

Participants in the futures market consist of hedgers and speculators. *Hedgers* seek to reduce the risk of price volatility from holding a position in the underlying asset by taking the opposite position in the futures market. For example, hedge transactions can be used to protect against changes in interest rates, changes in a stockmarket index or changes in individual share prices. Large companies, banks, life insurance companies and similar organisations face huge risks if commodity prices, interest rates or share prices change unexpectedly. They use futures to hedge against unexpected changes and thereby protect themselves against these risks.

Speculators accept the risk of price volatility in an attempt to profit from correctly anticipating future movements in commodity prices, interest rates or share prices. Although their role is often misunderstood, speculators are essential for the efficient operation of a futures market because their willingness to assume risk provides the means for hedgers to transfer it. Speculation in futures markets can be highly profitable. It is also very risky and a speculator should only risk money that they can afford to lose.

When you buy or sell a futures contract, you are actually trading the obligation to take delivery (if you are the buyer) or to make delivery (if you are the seller) of the underlying asset at a specific time in the future for the price that was agreed when the trade took place. However, futures contracts are rarely delivered because they are closed out by the purchase or sale of equal and opposite contracts. Moreover, many of the underlying financial instruments are notional, which means that they don't actually exist and delivery can only be made in cash.

The greatest volume of trading on the SFE is in financial futures. Financial futures can be divided into interest rate futures and equity futures. The leading interest rate futures consist of 90-day bank bill futures, three-year bond futures and ten-year bond futures. These correspond to short-term, medium-term and long-term interest rates. The leading equity futures consist of share price index futures and share futures.

Ninety-day bank bill futures

Bank accepted bills of exchange (bank bills) are negotiable debt securities that are sold at a discount for periods that are generally between 30 and 180 days. A bank bill represents a promise to pay the full face value on maturity and is backed by the credit rating of the bank that has accepted or guaranteed its repayment. Ninety-day bank bill futures provide traders with the means to take a position in anticipation of fluctuations in short-term interest rates. The bank bill contract represents an agreement to borrow or lend money for 90 days from a future date at an interest rate agreed upon today. The 90-day bank bill futures contract consists of the following terms.

If 90-day bank bill interest rates rise, then the value of bank bills will fall. Conversely, if 90-day bank bill interest rates decline, then the value of bank bills will increase. Therefore, if you are anticipating a *rise* in 90-day bank bill interest rates, then you will go *short* bank bill futures. On the other hand, if you think there will be a *decline* in 90-day bank bill interest rates, then you will go *long* bank bill futures.

Three-year bond futures

Three-year bond futures provide traders with the means to hedge against or speculate on fluctuations in medium-term interest rates. They are based on a notional three-year Commonwealth treasury bond with a coupon rate of 6 per cent. Since the underlying bonds don't actually exist, these futures contracts can only be settled with an equivalent sum in cash. The three-year bond futures contract consists of the following terms.

If medium-term interest rates rise, then the value of three-year bonds will fall. Similarly, if medium-term interest rates fall, then the value of three-year bonds will rise. Therefore, a trader anticipating a rise in medium-term interest rates will go short three-year bond futures, whereas a trader anticipating a decline in medium-term interest rates will go long three-year bond futures.

Ten-year bond futures

Ten-year bond futures provide traders with the means to hedge against or speculate on fluctuations in long-term interest rates. They are based on a notional ten-year Commonwealth treasury bond with a coupon rate of 6 per cent. Since the underlying bonds don't actually exist, these futures contracts can only be settled with an equivalent sum in cash. The ten-year bond futures contract consists of the following terms.

If long-term interest rates rise, then the value of ten-year bonds will fall. Similarly, if long-term interest rates decline, then the value of ten-year bonds will increase. Therefore, a trader anticipating a rise in long-term interest rates will go short ten-year bond futures, whereas a trader anticipating a decline in long-term interest rates will go long ten-year bond futures.

Share Price Index futures

Share Price Index (SPI) futures enable traders to hedge against or speculate on broad movements in the stockmarket as represented by the ASX200 Index. The ASX200 Index is equivalent to a diversified portfolio. Since the ASX200 Index does not physically exist, SPI futures contracts can only be settled with an equivalent sum in cash. A trader anticipating a rise in the index will go long SPI futures, whereas a trader anticipating a decline in the index will go short SPI futures.

Share futures

Futures contracts on the shares of a few listed public companies provide an alternative to trading in the underlying shares, ASXD equity options and warrants. Share futures can replicate a long or a short position in the underlying shares for hedging, asset allocation and trading strategies. So far, share futures have not been as popular as the SFE had hoped. The disadvantage of trading share futures is low trading volume, resulting in lack of liquidity.

Futures options

Futures options are puts and calls on futures contracts. They are American-style options that can be exercised at any time before expiry. Futures options are available on 90-day bank bill contracts, three-year treasury bond contracts, ten-year treasury bond contracts and SPI contracts. Premiums are quoted in the same terms as the underlying futures contract. Aside from leverage, the main advantage for trading futures options is the way in which the profit profile differs.

Futures trading

The main participants on the SFE are the members, who are predominantly banks, investment houses and stockbrokers who have direct access to the exchange to trade on behalf of themselves and their clients. Trading takes place on SYCOM, a screen-based dealing system that is also linked to major markets overseas. SYCOM terminals are located in each member's office and connected to a host computer at the SFE. SYCOM orders are matched on the basis of priority for price and time.

An opening position in a futures contract may be either *bought long* (anticipating a rise in the futures price) or *sold short* (anticipating a fall in the futures price). To *close out* a futures position, you trade in the opposite direction. For example, if you are long a futures contract, you simply sell a contract to close out your position. If you are short a futures contract, then you buy a contract to close out your position. You don't need to worry about who you bought from or sold to, because the SFE Clearing House stands between the parties to a transaction.

There are a number of ways in which you can instruct your broker to execute an order to buy or sell futures contracts. A *market order* is executed immediately at the current market bid or offer price. An order *at best* is similar to a market order except that it confers more discretion in terms of time and the manner of execution. A *limit order* tells your broker the maximum price you are willing to pay for a buy order or the minimum price you will accept for a sell order. An order *at discretion* is like a limit order, but it also gives the broker some discretion to vary the price if it is needed to fill the order. A *stop order*, or *stop-loss order*, tells the broker to trigger an order if the price reaches a certain level. Once triggered, it may be a market order or a limit order. A *market at close* order must be executed at the end of the trading session. A *spread order* is one in which one futures contract is bought and a different futures contract is simultaneously sold if the difference in their prices (the spread) is met.

You are required to put up a deposit for each new contract position, known as an *initial margin*. The amount of the initial margin is determined by the Clearing House and depends on the price volatility of the underlying asset. It provides the Clearing House with security to cover the credit risk of a party defaulting on a contact. The initial margin is repaid on delivery or when the contract position is closed out.

In addition to the initial margin, there is a *variation margin* which reflects movements in the futures price. You are required to pay the variation margin whenever the futures price moves against you. Failure to meet a margin call will automatically result in your position being closed out by your broker. You receive a variation margin credit whenever the futures price moves in your favour. You can withdraw the credit in cash. This whole process is called *mark to market* and its purpose is to maintain the balance of the initial margin. Other than margin requirements and brokerage fees, no further payments are made unless delivery takes place.

10

Managed investments

WHY MANAGED INVESTMENTS? 157
INVESTMENT STRATEGIES 158
UNIT TRUST PRODUCTS 162
INSURANCE PRODUCTS 163
SUPERANNUATION PRODUCTS 165
COST OF MANAGED INVESTMENTS 167
MONITORING PERFORMANCE 169

A managed investment is a pool of funds that is professionally administered on behalf of individual investors. It is a means by which individuals can invest *indirectly* in shares, interest-bearing securities and property. In Australia, the past decade has seen a dramatic expansion of managed investments as a result of the massive increase in superannuation savings.

Fund managers are skilled professionals whose objective is to enhance the wealth of investors. They undertake the process of selecting what investments to make and when to trade. They have access to the resources needed to research and analyse individual investments, gauge economic trends and make investment decisions. They offer economies of scale and diversification through a single investment. They make no promises, however, about the results they will achieve on your behalf.

The managed investments industry consists of a diverse group of institutions offering a variety of investment products. There are roughly 3000 investment products offered in Australia by 125 fund managers. They generally appear in one of three forms:

- *Unit trust products*—pooled investments that enable individuals to invest indirectly in shares, bonds, property, international investments and cash.
- *Life insurance products*—insurance bonds, friendly society bonds and annuities that enable individuals to invest indirectly in a similar range of securities.
- *Superannuation products*—employer-sponsored schemes, industry schemes, rollover funds and personal superannuation funds based on unit trust products and life insurance products.

The managed funds market is divided into a wholesale sector and a retail sector. The wholesale sector promotes itself to superannuation funds, government agencies and companies that can meet the minimum investment, which is usually $500 000. The retail sector serves individual or personal investors and accommodates minimum investments of as little as $500. The purpose of this chapter is to examine the retail sector for managed investments. It looks at reasons for and against indirect investing, the variety of managed investment strategies and the types of managed investment products. The chapter concludes with a discussion about the intermediaries who sell managed investment products.

The reason that many investors are attracted to managed investments is because they expect the fund manager to perform better than they would as direct investors. Unfortunately, investors expect more than fund managers can usually deliver. Very few investment managers consistently beat the market over the longer term, and the fee structure for a managed investment can amount to a significant reduction in your returns.

Why managed investments?

Is it better to put your money under professional management or invest it yourself? According to an ASX Shareownership Survey, approximately 40 per cent of Australian adults own shares either directly or indirectly. About 15 per cent invest directly, 12 per cent invest indirectly, and 13 per cent invest both directly and indirectly. What this means is that there is no clear consensus among Australian investors about the best way to invest.

Table 10.1 presents reasons given by investors who invest indirectly. It is clear that they prefer managed investments because they don't have the confidence to make their own investment decisions. They expect a managed investment to provide them with greater safety and less personal involvement than direct investing.

There are reasons for and against investing in managed funds. The benefits include professional expertise, diversity and less demand on your time. The drawbacks include extra costs and average performance. Choosing to invest indirectly depends on how you view the tradeoff between the investment performance you want and the amount of effort you are prepared to put into it.

Investment strategies

A managed fund has a set of objectives that guide the way in which it operates. These objectives form the foundation for the fund manager's investment strategy. Some funds follow very

Table 10.1 Reasons for managed investments

	Frequency
Security/safer	33.8
Need experts to manage investments	18.1
On advice from financial adviser	17.6
Lack of knowledge of sharemarket	15.3
Wanted long-term investment/growth	10.2
Spreads risk/good distribution of stocks	5.5
Don't have the time to dabble	5.4
Gift/inheritance	3.6
Lost money on direct shareownership	1.0

Source: ASX Australian Shareownership Survey

conservative strategies, some are balanced and others are more aggressive. The diversity of fund strategies enables you to find a managed investment product that matches your investment philosophy.

Cash management funds are an attractive alternative to holding short-term deposits in bank accounts that earn little or no interest. They invest in short-term money market securities such as bank accepted bills, treasury notes and interest-bearing deposits. The maturity period for most investments is less than 90 days, so they closely track the yields in the short-term money market. An investment in a cash management fund is virtually at call, with some also offering cheque access.

Capital guaranteed funds may invest in the full range of assets but generally limit the proportion of shares and property in the portfolio and invest mostly in debt securities. The returns are modest, but the original investment plus declared earnings are *guaranteed*. This type of fund is particularly suitable for cautious investors who want security of their capital or who have a short investment horizon.

Fixed interest funds are also called *income* funds or *bond* funds. They invest in debt securities issued or guaranteed by the Commonwealth, state or local governments and their statutory authorities, as well as corporate debt securities, mortgages and preference shares. The maturity of fixed interest fund investments is generally medium to long-term. Their objectives are a high interest yield with some profit from trading activity as a result of changes in interest rates.

Mortgage funds loan money on secured and registered first mortgages over real estate. They also invest in some fixed interest securities for liquidity. The interest rates on the mortgages may be fixed or variable. The returns from mortgage funds tend to be more stable than cash management funds and fixed interest funds. Short-term fluctuations in interest rates also have less impact.

Property funds differ according to the type of property (commercial, retail, industrial, residential or tourism) and its location (central business district, outer urban growth area or suburban shopping centre). Property funds have an income component and a growth component. If the fund borrows in order to maximise growth, then the income component will be reduced in order to pay the interest on the borrowings. Depending on the manager's strategy, a property fund may be targeting high income and low growth, balanced income and growth, or low income and high growth. A *split* property fund offers separate income investment and growth investment.

Diversified funds invest in the full range of securities, including money market securities, fixed interest securities, property and shares. Diversified funds include stable funds, balanced funds and growth funds.

- Diversified *stable* funds, sometimes called *Multi Sector 30*, are designed to achieve a reasonable level of capital stability. Capital stability means minimising the chance of negative returns over a twelve-month period. Investments are predominantly in short-term money market securities and fixed interest securities. Equity exposure is usually limited to 30 per cent of the portfolio.
- Diversified *balanced* funds, sometimes called *Multi Sector 50*, may have approximately equal investments in shares, property, fixed interest and money market securities. The proportions vary considerably, however, depending on the fund manager's views on timing and asset allocation. Equity exposure is usually limited to 50 per cent of the portfolio. Investors in balanced funds expect a moderate return over the medium term with the possibility of negative returns in some years.
- Diversified *growth* funds, sometimes called *Multi Sector 70* or *Multi Sector 70+*, concentrate up to 70 per cent of the portfolio in shares and property. Investors in growth funds expect moderate to high returns over the longer term. However, they are also exposed to higher levels of short-term volatility and risk.
- *Equity funds* invest in Australian shares. The investment strategies pursued by individual funds vary enormously. Equity funds that emphasise *growth* are exposed to greater risk by investing in particular market sectors such as resource shares or special situations. Equity funds that emphasise *income* stick to high-yielding blue chip shares, shares paying fully franked dividends and preference shares. A number of specialised funds can be found among this group.

- *Industrial funds* invest in the larger Australian industrial shares with a view to steady growth over the longer term.
- *Resource funds* invest in the shares of mining and petroleum companies with a view to strong growth over the longer term.
- *Small cap funds* invest in the shares of smaller companies (small capitalisation) with a view to strong potential growth.
- *Socially responsible investment funds* (SRI), sometimes called 'ethical investments', avoid investing in companies involved in businesses such as alcohol, tobacco, armaments, gambling or uranium, and give preference to companies that contribute to the community, protect the environment and adopt responsible workplace practices.
- *Special situation funds* invest in the shares of companies that are in circumstances that may lead to a substantial gain, such as a takeover.
- *Imputation funds* invest in companies that pay fully franked dividends.
- *Index funds* invest in a selection of shares that replicate the performance of a stockmarket index such as the All Ordinaries Index.
- *Property securities funds* invest in the shares of listed property funds.

Overseas funds are generally managed locally by a manager with overseas links. The purpose is to gain exposure to securities in other countries. The globalisation of the securities markets, together with the advantages of international diversification, have increased the popularity of overseas funds. Overseas funds may invest in debt securities, equity securities, property and currencies. Most of the emphasis, however, has been on growth and emerging markets. Overseas funds may spread their investments around the world, or they may target specific regions such as America, Europe, Japan or the Pacific basin. Overseas funds carry the additional risk of changes in the exchange rate between the Australian dollar and the currencies in which overseas investments are made. Most of this risk can be hedged. For these reasons, the expenses associated with managing international investments are a bit higher.

Index funds are managed passively. The fund manager is not trying to beat the index. Instead, they pick a representative sample of investments that tracks the benchmark index. The main advantage is that the fund is less expensive to run. A fund that can match the average returns of its benchmark index and operate with a lower cost is likely to produce better returns than many of its contemporaries. However, if you invest in an index fund, it means that you are not only satisfied with average returns, but also are content to let the fund manager abdicate responsibility for asset selection or investment timing.

Hedge funds invest in a variety of assets, including overseas securities. Their main claim is that they are managed so that their returns are not *correlated* to returns in other investment products or the market. They achieve this by diversification and a range of *hedging* devices such as short selling, options, futures and warrants.

Unit trust products

A unit trust may be listed or unlisted. A *listed trust* sells a fixed number of shares to investors in a public offering that is similar to the float of a new company. The proceeds of the issue are used to invest in other securities. The shares are traded on the ASX and the price fluctuates according to supply and demand. Since the number of shares on issue is fixed, listed trusts are referred to as *closed-end* funds.

Unlisted trust units are not traded on the ASX. They are sold by the unit trust on the basis of a prospectus. The price of a unit depends upon its *net asset value* (NAV). NAV consists of the value of the investment portfolio divided by the number of units outstanding. NAV, therefore, fluctuates according to changes in the prices of the investments in the trust portfolio. An unlisted trust is referred to as an *open-end* fund because it provides a continuous offering and redemption of units. Some unlisted unit trusts, however, are closed to new investors. The majority of unit trusts are unlisted and they cover every type of investment strategy.

The fund manager promotes the sale of units through intermediaries and manages the fund according to a Constitution that sets down the rights, responsibilities, policies and procedures. The manager must be a corporation and must have a securities dealer's licence issued by the ASIC. A third party acts as custodian of the trust assets on behalf of the unit-holders. The law requires the manager to provide regular reports to the unit holders, including a review of the investment operations and financial details of the trust. They are also required to submit financial statements and associated reports with the ASIC.

A prospectus is required by the Corporations Law and must be approved by the ASIC. The main function of the prospectus is to ensure that any offer to invest in a trust is based on information that is accurate, but it does not guarantee that the investment will be profitable. The prospectus is potentially the most important piece of information that you have with which to judge a unit trust. Discovering what a fund manager really means and whether this approach is actually put into practice is an essential ingredient in matching a unit trust with your investment goals. Watch out for managers that fail to clearly articulate their investment philosophy in the prospectus.

It is a legal requirement that an application for the purchase of units in an unlisted trust be detached from a currently registered prospectus. If the prospectus expires and a new prospectus is not registered, then the trust is closed to new investors. The procedures for calculating the buying and selling price and the manager's obligation to redeem units are described in the prospectus.

A unit trust is not a tax entity and pays no tax itself. However, it must distribute all of its income and capital gains to the unit-holders each year and they pay tax on their distributions. A unit trust can also pass on tax credits such as dividend imputation credits or depreciation benefits from property investments.

Insurance products

A life insurance company invests directly in assets as part of its *statutory funds*. This arrangement makes life insurance products different from unit trusts. Instead of a prospectus, they only require a customer information brochure. The life insurance company manages the investment portfolio itself and acts as the custodian of the assets. Life insurance products are tax-paid investments. This means that the insurance company pays tax on the income and realised capital gains. Insurance investment products consist of insurance bonds, friendly society bonds and immediate annuities.

An *insurance bond* is a single premium life insurance policy. The name *bond* is misleading because these are not bonds at all. They are investment-linked life insurance policies that serve the same function as a unit trust except in a different legal context. The insurance company pays tax on investment income and capital gains. You receive no distributions because interest, dividends and capital gains are reinvested. If you hold an insurance bond for ten years, you won't pay tax on the profits realised on redemption. If you redeem it early, there are exit fees and tax liabilities. Insurance bonds are predominantly capital-guaranteed and capital-stable funds.

There has been a drift away from insurance bonds as a result of changes in Department of Social Security deeming regulations and poor overall performance. However, since the superannuation surcharge came into effect, there has been some renewed interest in insurance bonds because the earnings are reinvested and they don't declare any taxable income from a bond. This helps some high-income earners to get their taxable income below the superannuation surcharge threshold.

Friendly societies began collecting money for sick benefits and funerals as far back as 1830. *Friendly society bonds* are similar to insurance bonds, although the range of investment strategies is somewhat restricted compared with insurance bonds. Most friendly societies outsource their fund management.

You can buy an *immediate annuity* from an insurance company for a lump sum payment. The annuity entitles you to receive an income stream from the insurance company. The payments can be for your lifetime or for a fixed period up to 25 years. The amount of the payment is stipulated in the annuity contract and depends on the term of the annuity and the insurer's views about interest rates. The payments consist of a return of capital component and an income component. The return of capital component is not taxable but the income component is taxed at your marginal rate. Some annuities index the payments to compensate for inflation, and others pay the residual capital value to your beneficiary if you die before the end of the term.

Superannuation products

Superannuation schemes consist of employer-sponsored schemes and personal schemes. There are a number of tax advantages associated with investing in a superannuation scheme. However, you should get expert tax advice on superannuation because it is not only complicated, but also subject to continuing amendment by the Commonwealth government. Superannuation is a long-term investment that cannot be withdrawn until you retire.

An employer-sponsored superannuation scheme is one established by an employer into which only the employer or their employees may contribute. These schemes may be administered internally by the employer organisation. Because of their complexity, however, employer superannuation schemes are often administered by external fund managers. In addition to employer-sponsored superannuation funds, a number of industry superannuation funds have been established by trade unions and employer groups in order to receive contributions that are required under industrial awards and the Superannuation Guarantee Scheme. Most industry funds are administered by external fund managers.

Personal superannuation schemes have also been established by most fund managers. They are offered to individuals who cannot contribute to an employer-sponsored scheme or who wish to supplement their employer-sponsored superannuation. An employer can make contributions directly to a fund nominated by the employee.

Superannuation products are designed to take advantage of tax concessions offered to people who are saving for their retirement. A concessional tax rate of 15 per cent is paid on contributions into these funds and on the investment income earned by them. This means that most of the tax is deferred until you retire, when your marginal tax rate may be lower. For individuals on high incomes, however, a further superannuation surcharge of up to 15 per cent makes personal superannuation contributions somewhat less attractive. Personal superannuation managed investments are available as unit trust products and insurance products.

A *Superannuation Trust* is a unit trust that is designed specifically to comply with superannuation legislation. It can receive rollover payments from other superannuation funds, eligible termination payments as a result of leaving a job and direct contributions. Benefits can be paid as a lump sum or as a superannuation pension when you retire.

An *Approved Deposit Fund* (ADF) is a rollover fund that can be used if you leave one superannuation fund and you want to preserve your benefits within the superannuation system until you retire. ADFs can only receive eligible termination payments. They are invested until you are 65 years of age, when they must be withdrawn as a lump sum.

A *Superannuation Bond* is an insurance bond that is designed to comply with superannuation legislation. It can receive rollover payments, eligible termination payments and direct contributions. Benefits are paid as a lump sum when you retire at age 65.

A *Deferred Annuity* (DA) is a rollover fund that can be used if you leave one superannuation fund and you want to preserve your benefits within the superannuation system until you retire. DAs can only receive eligible termination payments. They are invested until you are 65 years of age, when they must be withdrawn as an *annuity*.

Allocated superannuation products are post-retirement products. They enable you to invest a lump sum superannuation payout into a pension account so that you not only have a regular income, but also defer the tax on investment earnings that you might otherwise pay. To receive the tax concessions, you need to comply with minimum and maximum income payments prescribed by the government. *Allocated pensions* are unit trust products and *allocated annuities* are insurance products.

The income payments consist of investment earnings and some return of your capital. They are taxed similarly to an immediate annuity. One of the features that makes allocated products attractive is the degree of control you can retain. For example, if you are planning an overseas trip, you can elect to make a lump sum withdrawal. You can also vary the income payments within the minimum and maximum limits. The balance in your account depends on investment earnings, lump sum withdrawals and income payments. The benefits continue as long as there are enough funds in the account.

Do-it-yourself or self-managed superannuation funds are the fastest growing segment of the superannuation industry. Running your own superannuation fund involves a tremendous amount of effort and expense in order to comply with the regulations that govern administration and investment policy. However, the cost may be rewarded in terms of tax savings and control over your retirement investments.

Cost of managed investments

Investors in managed investments are subject to a number of costs that don't apply to direct investing. Some fees are paid directly by the investor and some are paid indirectly by the fund. The fees may include a cost to purchase units, called an *entry fee*, a cost for managing the fund, called a *management fee*, and a cost to redeem units, called an *exit fee*. The prospectus for unit trust products and the customer information brochure for insurance products explain the fees.

Entry fees

Most funds charge an entry fee when units are purchased that is usually between 3 per cent and 5 per cent of the amount invested. It is also called a *front-end fee*, a *contribution fee* or an *establishment fee*. A substantial part of the entry fee is paid as a commission to the brokers, financial advisers and financial planners who sell managed investments. Cash management trusts and mortgage trusts don't charge an entry fee.

In addition to the entry fee, there may be an additional cost called the *buy/sell spread*. This is the difference between the buying price and the selling price, and it can range from 0.4 per cent to 1.4 per cent of the amount invested. The reason for the buy/sell spread is the stamp duty and brokerage costs that the fund incurs as people enter and leave the fund. These costs are sometimes added to the price when you are buying and subtracted from the price when you are selling—resulting in a difference between the two prices.

A fund manager may also be paying a continuing commission to the investment adviser for as long as the investment is not redeemed. These commissions are variously called *ongoing*, *trailing*, *volume*, *servicing* and *dividend reinvestment* commissions. They are typically in the range of 0.5 per cent to 1.0 per cent per year.

A growing number of fund managers are developing alternative channels of distribution that enable investors to save money on entry fees. If you know what you want and don't ask for advice, there are discount brokers that rebate between 75 and 100 per cent of the initial fee and 50 per cent of the continuing fees. Some rebates can be taken in cash and others in additional units. For example, a 5 per cent entry fee typically includes a 1 per cent manager's fee and a 4 per cent initial commission. If the discount broker rebates 80 per cent of the initial commission, it means that they will rebate 3.2 per cent and you will pay only 1.8 per cent of the amount invested.

The entry fee is a big problem for the managed investments industry. It deters many investors from putting their money under management. For this reason, expect to see increasing numbers of *no-load* funds appearing in the Australian market. However, watch out for no-load funds that try to claw back the entry fee with higher management fees and exit fees.

Management fees

Management fees are regularly deducted from managed investments. These fees and other expenses are required to be fully disclosed, but sometimes they are not always easy to identify. The issue of fees and charges becomes even more complex with master trusts and wrap accounts.

- The investment manager charges an annual management fee that will range from 0.25 per cent to 2 per cent of the value of the assets under management.
- There are also expenses to recover running costs such as stamp duty, auditors' fees, trustee fees, custodian fees, interest expense, bank charges, postage and printing.
- Some funds also allow the manager to charge an additional fee based on performance.

The overall cost of operating a managed investment is measured by the *management expense ratio* (MER). This is the total annual management fees and recoverable expenses paid out of the fund expressed as a percentage of the fund's average value. The MER does not include brokerage costs, which may be considerable for an active fund manager with high turnover, nor does it include capital gains taxes paid directly by the fund.

MERs for retail funds in Australia generally range from 1 per cent to 3 per cent, with the average around 2 per cent. There is evidence that MERs for Australian managed investments are high compared with similar funds overseas. There is no evidence that funds with higher MERs consistently deliver better performance.

Exit fees

To redeem units in an unlisted fund, the unit-holder sends an application to the fund manager who is obliged to buy the units back within a prescribed time. A number of funds charge an exit fee on redemption. Others charge an exit fee that is based on a sliding scale depending on how long your money was under management. Many funds don't charge an exit fee. There are no exit fees for listed trusts except for normal brokerage fees.

Monitoring performance

Past performance is the factor that most influences investors and advisers in the selection of managed investments. However, the past can be a very poor guide to future performance. The track record for most fund managers suggests that consistent superior performance is difficult to achieve. Each asset class performs differently at various stages of the business cycle. Superior performance not only depends on superior asset selection, but also on superior timing. Most fund managers do a credible job of asset selection. Not even the best fund managers, however, are consistently superior at forecasting changes in interest rates or predicting major turning points in the stockmarket.

Another reason why so many fund managers turn in an average performance is because it is in their interest to play it safe. A manager's performance is compared with a benchmark such as the All Ordinaries Index. If the manager's performance falls behind the benchmark, then investors will leave the fund and invest in other funds. If the manager tries to beat the benchmark, they run a greater risk that they may fail. So they invest cautiously in a selection of securities that does not stray too far from the benchmark profile. It is known in the industry that many 'active' managers are more conservative than they claim to be.

The investment management industry is very sensitive about performance figures that include the effects of entry and exit fees. They prefer to quote *gross performance* figures that don't include deductions for entry fees and exit fees. Gross performance figures reflect the investment performance of the fund, but they overstate the actual returns to individual investors who have paid fees.

What managed fund performance figures routinely fail to disclose is the *after-tax* effect of their investment decisions. Fund managers are most concerned with gross performance figures and give little thought to their investors' after-tax returns. Consequently, investors sometimes find themselves paying substantial taxes as a result of their fund manager's 'active' trading policies.

Published information

There are a number of sources of published performance information for managed investments. Figure 10.1 is an example of the *Personal Investor/Assirt Performance Tables*.

- Gross performance is reported as the percentage rate of return over one year, three years and five years.
- The *Quartiles* column ranks the fund's performance for each of the past four successive twelve-month periods within its category. A quartile ranking of 1 means that the performance was in the top 25 per cent of similar funds and a ranking of 4 means that it was in the bottom 25 per cent of similar funds. Therefore, a fund with quartile rankings of 2222 is more consistent than a fund with quartile rankings of 1414.
- *Volatility* is the Assirt percentile ranking.

Figure 10.1 Personal Investor/Assirt PerformanceTables

Equity trusts

Fund Name (*= closed fund)	Price	Gross performance 1 yr %	3 yrs %	5 yrs %	Quartilies	Volatility	Cash	Entry fee	Size ($m)
Kingston Equity Trust	3.9700	12.40	6.06	9.87	4234	82	4	5.0	34

- The *Cash* column reports the percentage of the fund's assets held in cash.
- *Entry fee* is the maximum entry fee charged.
- *Size* of the fund is the total value of the fund assets in $million.

Fund reports

Reports to members are another source of performance information. The quality of these reports says much about the quality of the fund manager. Members' reports should include the following information:

- General commentary on the financial markets.
- Performance data for the fund, together with an analysis of the portfolio's performance against its benchmark.
- The manager's outlook and strategy for the next period.
- Details about the assets held, their valuation, income received, distributions paid and the costs of managing the fund.
- Financial statements.

The most important source of performance information is your account statement. It tells you what happened to your investment. Your results can be different from the fund's overall results if you enter or exit the fund during the fund's financial year. An informative account statement ought to contain the following information:

- The number of units that you held at the beginning and the end of the reporting period, including any purchases or redemptions.
- The value of a unit at the beginning and the end of the reporting period.
- The total dollar value of your holding at the beginning and the end of the reporting period.
- Details of investment returns, including the returns from capital gains and the returns from income.
- A comparison of the fund's performance relative to its benchmark.
- The dollar value of all fees and charges levied against your account.

It is not likely that you will get an account statement containing this much detail. Most funds are notoriously inept at disclosing details about performance and fees. The ASIC has criticised the lack of disclosure in account statements and asked the industry to make improvements. If you want this type of disclosure, ask to see a sample account statement before you invest your money.

Research organisations

There are a number of research organisations that analyse the practices and performance of managed investments in Australia. They sell this information to financial advisers and in some cases to individual investors. If you want to sift through the countless Australian managed investments that are on the market, these organisations are in the business of making the task easier. However, there is always much controversy about which organisation has the best methodology and the most reliable ratings. Here are some examples.

- *Assirt* http://www.assirt.com.au offers research reports and computer software to fund managers and financial planners. Assirt performance data is regularly published in financial periodicals such as *Personal Investment* magazine.
- *InvestorWeb* http://www.investorweb.com.au provides comprehensive information about managed investments which it

sells directly to individual investors. Its star rating system is for funds, rather than fund managers.

- *Morningstar Research* http://www.morningstar.com.au (formerly FPG Research) provides information for unlisted funds in Australia and New Zealand for governments, financial planners, fund managers and investors. It is best known for its 'star' rating system.
- *Van Eyk Research* http://www.vaneyk.com.au evaluates a range of fund managers. They describe their rating system as 'opinionated'.

The methods used by each research organisation vary tremendously. The funds or the fund managers are rated by stars, letters or symbols. The researchers look at the manager's operations, experience, investor safeguards, minimising risk and maximising returns. They sell reports in which they publish their ratings and in some cases make recommendations such as 'strong buy', 'buy', 'hold' or 'sell'. Financial planners use this information to select funds that meet the risk profile of their clients. Individual investors can use the same information to decide for themselves.

Picking a fund

When you have decided upon your preferred investment strategy, the following approach will help you to select a fund from among the candidates. The objective is to select the top-performing, most highly rated and lowest-cost fund in which to invest.

- Make a list of all the funds that pursue an investment strategy that matches your investment philosophy.
- Remove those funds that performed poorly over the past few years. While past performance is not a guarantee of future performance, some research suggests that funds with superior performance are more likely to continue to perform well in the near term.
- Look for the funds that have the highest ratings from one of the research organisations such as Assirt or Morningstar.
- Look for the funds that have the lowest management expense ratio.

Now you have a shortlist of top-performing, highly rated, low-cost candidates that are suited to your investment strategy. The last step is to look for a stockbroker or financial planner who will help you to choose one or two funds in which to invest and who will offer you a generous rebate on the entry fee.

Index

account, 5, 55–7,
active investing, 28, 131
advance-decline line, 102
All Ordinaries Index, 34
allocated products, 166
annual report, 38, 171
approved deposit fund, 166
asset allocation, 24–5
Australian Securities and Investments Commission (ASIC), 15, 163
Australian Stock Exchange, 7, 43–5

balance sheet, *see* statement of financial position
balanced strategy, 29–30
bar chart, 104–5
beta, 68–9, 97
Black-Scholes Option Pricing Model, 140
bond, *see* debt securities
bonus issue, 74
business cycle, 25–6, 76
buy-and-hold strategy, 130
buyback, 72–3

call option, 141–2, 144–5
candlestick chart, 106
Capital Asset Pricing Model, 97
capital gain, 66–74
capital gains tax, 13
cash cow, 70–1
cash flow, *see* statement of cash flow
charting, 103–111
CHESS, 8–9
company, 78–9
contract note, 8
convertible note, 121
credit rating, 125–6

data, 116
debt securities, 2, 117–33
decision rule, 26
deferred annuity, 166
delta, 138
derivative, 3, 134–55
discount securities, 119–20
discount yield, 123, 131–3
diversification, 26–7
dividend, 64–5, 92–3
dividend imputation, 13–14

earnings, 72, 80–3, 93–6
economic clock, 25–6
Elliott wave theory, 108
entry fee, 167–8
equity option, 135–47
equity securities, 2, 58–74
exercise price, 135–6
exit fee, 169

fees, 5, 167–9
Fibonacci numbers, 108
financial planner, 9–11
financial ratios, 86–95
Financial Services Reform Act, 15
financial statements, 79–95
fixed interest securities, 120–1
float, 71
franking credit, 14
fundamental analysis, 66–7, 75–98
fund strategy, 158–62
futures contract, 150–5

Gann analysis, 108–9
genetic algorithm, 113
goals, 18–19
growth strategy, 30, 66–74

high-low index, 102–3

income statement, *see* statement of financial performance
income strategy, 29, 64–5
index, 33–5
industry sector, 76–7
information, 33–46, 170–4
insurance bond, 163–4
interest rates, 127–30
Internet, 40–1, 47–57
investment strategy, 24–31, 158–62
investor protection, 14–15
issuer sponsored holding, 9

laddering, 131
liquidity, 27–8, 90–2, 125–6

MACD, 110–11
magazines, 35–7
managed investment, 3, 156–74
management, 72
management expense ratio, 169
management fees, 168–9
margin, 155
market indicator, 102–103
master trust, 11–12
merger, *see* takeover
moving average, 109–11

neural network, 112
newspapers, 35–7

on-line investing, 47–57
operating performance, 86–90
option, 61, 135–47
order, 5–8, 154–5
ordinary share, 59–60
oscillator, 111
over-the-counter market, 7–8

passive investing, 28, 130–1
performance, 31–2, 78–9, 86–90, 169–74
point and figure chart, 106–7
preference share, 60–1
premium, 137
present value, 96–8
price-earnings ratio, 68, 96
profit and loss account, *see* statement of financial performance
prospectus, 38
put option, 142–3, 145–7

quotation, 62–3, 135–8

rate of return, 20–1, 121–3
research, 38–43, 172–4
return, *see* rate of return
rights, 61–2
risk, 21–4, 67–70, 123–7

settlement, 8–9
shares, *see* equity securities
short-term money market, 119–20
small company shares, 70, 71
software, 113–15
solvency, 90–2
speculative strategy, 31
split, 74
statement of cash flow, 84–6
statement of financial performance, 80–3
statement of financial position, 83–4
stockbroker, 3–5, 38–9, 47–57
strike price, 135–6
subscription service, 41–3
superannuation, 165–7
swap, 133
Sydney Futures Exchange, 7, 45–6, 154–5

takeover, 73–4
taxation, 12–14
technical analysis, 67, 99–116
thin capitalisation, 71
timing, 25–6

uncertainty, 21–4
under-valued assets, 72
unit trust, 162–3

value, 70–4, 92–8
volatility, 21–4, 69, 127–30, 137, 139–40
volume, 103

warrant, 147–50
World Wide Web, *see* Internet
wrap account, 12

yield curve, 127–9, 131–3
yield to maturity, 122–3

Going Solo in Your Own Small Business
John English

If you want to get into business on your own, this guide to the essentials of self-employment will help you turn your dream into reality.

From the author of the bestselling *How to Organise and Operate a Small Business in Australia* comes a handbook of practical, common-sense advice about how to start a solo business, and how to run it successfully. It will help you navigate your way through the most important aspects of being your own boss, but without weighing you down with lots of detail.

Going Solo in Your Own Small Business is also about discovering what you really want to get out of life, and how your work can be in harmony with the way you want to live. It's about more than being self-employed and getting paid for what you do – it's about the power of being small.

ISBN 1 86508 606 1

Printed in Dunstable, United Kingdom

88180802R00117